The author and publisher of this book respectfully acknowledge the Traditional Owners of the land we call Melbourne: the Wurundjeri Woi-wurrung and Bunurong/Boon wurrung peoples of the Kulin Nation. We pay respect to their Elders past and present and acknowledge and honour the unbroken spiritual, cultural and environmental connections they have maintained to this unique place for countless generations.

MELBOURNE MOMENTS

MELBOURNE MOMENTS

A compendium of fun facts and surprising stories from the 'marvellous' city

ANDREW WATSON

radiate

radiate

Radiate Publishing
Melbourne, Australia.

radiatepublishing@gmail.com
Facebook: Melbourne Moments
Instagram: melbournemoments_

First published 2024
Text © Andrew Watson 2024
Design and typography © Radiate Publishing 2024
Produced entirely in Melbourne, Australia

ISBN 978 0 6487055 9 8

All rights reserved. This book is copyrighted. Apart from any use permitted under the *Australian Copyright Act* 1968 and subsequent amendments, and any exceptions permitted under any current statutory licence scheme administered by officially authorised entities such as the Australian Copyright Agency, no part may be reproduced, stored in a retrieval system or transmitted by any means or process whatsoever or used in the development or use of artificial intelligence software or similar without the express, prior written permission of the publisher.

Photographs and illustrations in this book are credited where appropriate. Other photographs are the author's own or in the public domain or are included under provisions of a Creative Commons licence. No part, text, design, image or layout of this book was produced by means of artificial intelligence software.

Cover image: 'Digger's Wedding' by S. T. Gill, 1852. [*State Library of Victoria*]

 A catalogue record for this book is available from the National Library of Australia

Contents

Preface		ix
Map		xiv
1	**1802–1849**	1
	A village is established and quickly grows.	
2	**1850–1879**	17
	Gold makes many rich and the city booms.	
3	**1880–1899**	45
	The people are entertained, but things soon go bust.	
4	**1900–1939**	73
	War is declared. Motor transport arrives. Rogues and ruffians abound.	

| 5 | **1940–1999** | 107 |

Another war. Immigration surges. The city modernises and expands.

| 6 | **2000–2024** | 141 |

The city evolves and reaches upwards. Things go digital. Heritage in jeopardy.

Further reading   153

Index   156

Preface

In 1885, British journalist George Augustus Sala wrote about Australia in a series of lengthy articles titled *The Land of the Golden Fleece*. He delighted the citizens of Melbourne especially (well, most of them) by describing their city as admirable and "marvellous." The epithet stuck and has endured as part of Melbourne's 'brand' ever since.

Although he wrote mostly for the London *Daily Telegraph* and the *Illustrated London News*, Sala's articles were syndicated around the world. The following edited extracts, reproduced here by way of an introduction to the story of Melbourne from 1802 onwards, were first published as part of the *Golden Fleece* series in *The Argus* newspaper on 8 August 1885.

"I should explain why I have called Melbourne a marvellous city. The metropolis and seat of government of the colony of Victoria has at present, within a 10-mile radius, including the city and suburbs, a population of more than 282,000 souls. The rateable property in the city is valued at ten millions sterling, with a net annual value of nearly a million. The principal thoroughfares are a mile in length, 99 feet in width, and intersect each other at right angles. Omnibuses, hansoms, and hackney waggonettes swarm in the streets; and very soon an extensive system of horse-tramway cars will be thrown open.

"The Anglican and Roman [Catholic] Communions have splendid cathedrals, and there is a multitude of handsome and commodious places of worship for other denominations. The Town Hall is gigantic and imposing; the General Post Office vast, comely, and admirably arranged. There is a splendid university. Government House is not, perhaps, architecturally a thing of beauty which should live forever; still, it affords a spacious and dignified residence for His Excellency Sir Henry Loch and his lady.

"There are half a dozen theatres, more or less. There is a very grand permanent exhibition building and a fine aquarium. When the new Houses of Parliament are finished they will form a very sumptuous pile indeed. There is one thoroughly excellent and admirable hotel in Melbourne — Menzies' — and a few other far from uncomfortable caravanseries. There are asylums, markets, hospitals, coffee palaces, public and private schools, clubs, parks, gardens, race-courses, and recreation grounds in profusion in and about the city; and I need scarcely say that there are any number of big banks and insurance offices which, in their architecture, are more than palatial. The whole city, in short, teems with wealth, even as it does with humanity.

The first shipment of gold arrives at government offices in William Street, Melbourne, escorted by heavily armed troopers, 1852. [*State Library of Victoria*]

"Well, you might say, what is there wonderful in all this? Melbourne is the prosperous capital of a prosperous British Colony. What is there to marvel at in its possession of all, or nearly all, the features of the most advanced civilisation? But there is much that is marvellous in Melbourne. The city is not 50 years old. In the year 1836 — the year before Queen Victoria ascended the throne — the present site of Melbourne was known as Bearbrass. On Waterloo Day, 1836, there were just 13 buildings — three of weatherboard, two of slate, and eight turf hovels.

"Only the year before, one of the virtual founders of Melbourne, John Pascoe Fawkner, landed on the bush on the banks of the Yarra River, bringing with him a party of five men, together with two horses, two pigs, three kangaroo dogs, and a cat. Melbourne crept along, so to speak, until the year 1851, when the discovery of gold in the colony, and the consequent rush from all parts of the world to the diggings, suddenly transformed 'Bearbrass' into a mighty city. "God made the country, and man made the town," wrote Cowper. It was gold that made Melbourne!"

Sala goes on to mention seeing a lithograph depicting the arrival of the first gold escort into Melbourne and how, the following day, as news spread, many workers quit their job on the spot and headed to the goldfields. He concludes his article by acknowledging that gold — and the people who dug it out of the ground — had created a splendid, wealthy city, with many fine buildings and institutions.

"The consequence was that everybody, from all parts of the world, who had a little money, and a great deal more energy and pluck, started for the diggings. There was a proportion of weak-kneed brethren whose pluck vanished as quickly as their money did, but it soon became a case of the survival of the fittest. There was left a residuum of real 'live men,' as the Americans say, and those live men and their sons have made Melbourne what she is: magnificent and marvellous."

There have been many quirky, unlikely and occasionally unhappy episodes in the story of 'magnificent and marvellous' Melbourne since Batman and Fawkner raced to the swampy land at the mouth of the Yarra and began to build a village. This book contains some of those moments.

PREFACE | xiii

Doing The Block in Collins Street (page 31).
S. T. Gill, 1880. (*State Library of Victoria*)

Next page: map of the Bourke, Gipps and Lonsdale wards of the City of
Melbourne, effectively the grid designed by Robert Hoddle (page 8). Notable
features include Batman's Hill (page 8), the two railway stations, and the
large cemetery on the site of the present-day Victoria Market (page 42).
Stephen Street was later renamed Exhibition Street. Drawn by James
Kerney in 1855. [*State Library of Victoria*]

MAP | xv

John Batman, his journey along the Yarra, and a contemporary view of the new village. [*State Library of Victoria*]

1

1802–1849

A village is established
and quickly grows

SUSPICION AND ALARM

In January 1802, Philip Gidley King, Governor of the British colony based at Port Jackson (Sydney), became suspicious about the motives of French explorer Nicholas Baudin who had begun to map the coast close to what is now Wilson's Promontory. King decided to make haste to secure the area and His Majesty's Armed Survey Vessel *Lady Nelson*, already in Bass Strait on other duties, was assigned to the task.

LAND GRAB

Governor King's fears were well-founded: Baudin already considered the land to be *Terre Napoléon* and one of the other expedition leaders, François Péron, had sent First Consul (soon to be Emperor) Bonaparte a plan to invade and capture the poorly defended Port Jackson. Clearly, the French were just as keen as the British to expand their empire.

GOOD BAY VIEWS

On the morning of 14 February 1802, on board the *Lady Nelson*, Acting-Lieutenant John Murray crossed the treacherous rip and sailed into the wide expanse of water we now call Port Phillip

The *Lady Nelson* entering Port Phillip Bay, as imagined by C. Allen Green in about 1865. [*State Library of Victoria*]

Bay. He landed, sought fresh water, and climbed the first big hill he saw, naming it Arthur's Seat, after a vaguely similar hill in his native Edinburgh. He noted the distant shoreline, then sailed north to what is now Hobsons Bay.

NAKED TRUTH

There were unconfirmed reports that some indigenous tribespeople who met Murray refused to talk to him until he removed all his clothes, possibly to prove he was not female. It is not known if he complied.

BATMAN BEGINS

John Batman, probably the most influential figure in the founding of Melbourne, was born in New South Wales in January 1801 to William Batman, a transported convict. After an unfinished apprenticeship as a blacksmith (his master died), John left for Launceston, Van Dieman's Land (Tasmania), in 1821 with his brother Henry. In 1828 he married pardoned convict Eliza Thompson — who had previously been found guilty in London of passing a fake bank note — but only after the happy couple had received special permission to do so from Lieutenant-Governor George Arthur. Batman's life in Van Dieman's Land is the subject of much controversy because of his involvement in the so-called 'Black War' killings of Aboriginal people and the 'Black Line' episode during which Indigenous people were driven into a 'manageable' area.

THE PORT PHILLIP ASSOCIATION

In the midst of a burgeoning career as a property speculator and occasional government agent, Batman formed a syndicate with other entrepreneurs and in 1835 began to make claims for land around Port Phillip Bay. Hearing that a rival claimant, John Fawkner, was already *en route*, Batman raced him to the Bay in the *Rebecca*, anchoring at Indented Head, east of present-day Geelong, on 29 May.

NOT A PROPER TREATY

Batman's contentious — and later invalidated — treaty with the local indigenous people involved 'purchasing' 600 acres in return for 30 axes, 100 knives, 50 scissors, 40 blankets, 200 handkerchiefs, 100 pounds of flour, six shirts, and 30 mirrors. Historians believe that the Kulin elders with whom he negotiated did not intend to sell their land and thought they were agreeing to a temporary lease in return for an annual rent.

BAT(E)MAN

Batman wanted to call Melbourne 'Batmania' even though his family name may have once been spelled Bateman. Somewhere along the way the 'e' fell off, but 'Bateman' occasionally appears on official documents and plans.

A VILLAGE PEOPLE

Batman famously wrote "This will be the place for a village" after venturing along the Yarra River (which, naturally, he wanted to call the River Batman) but he appears to have been merely echoing the words of a previous explorer that the low waterfall close to what is now Queens Bridge — and where fresh water began — was the most suitable location for a settlement.

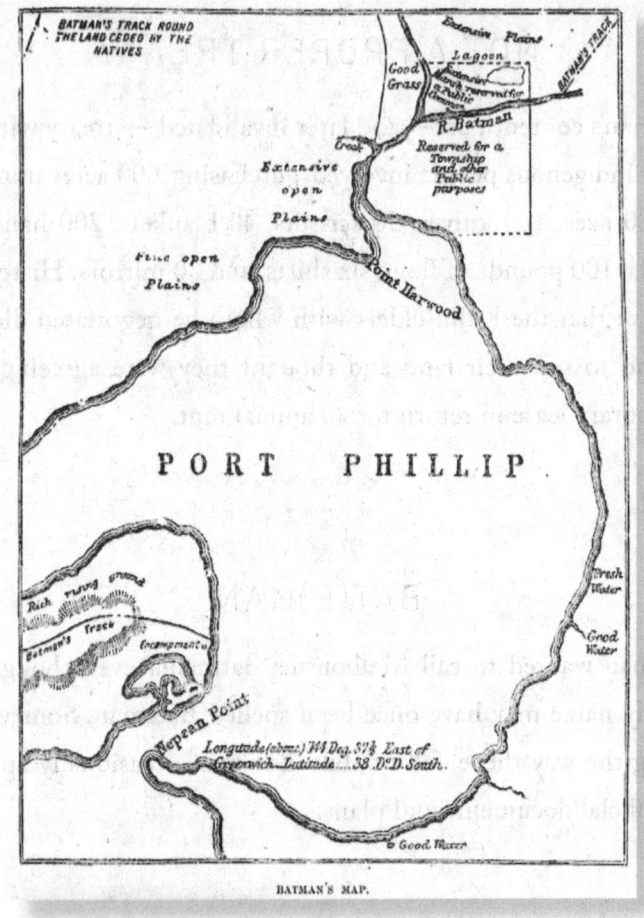

John Batman's first attempt at a map. [*State Library of Victoria*]

BEARBRASS AND BEARPORT

Despite wishful thinking by some superhero fans, 'Batmania' was only one of several names used for the new settlement. Another was 'Bearbrass', thought to be based on a mispronunciation of the name Birrarung, or 'river of mists' in the lan-

'A view from Bateman's Hill,' H. G. Jones, c.1841. [*State Library of Victoria*]

guage of the Wurundjeri people. Their term for the Yarra was 'Yarro-yarro' or 'ever-flowing.' Other names used then discarded include Bareport, Bareheep, Barehurp and Bareberp. In the end, Governor Bourke decided on 'Melbourne,' after the British Prime Minister at the time.

FLAT HILL

Batman built his family home in 1836 on Pleasant Hill which he renamed Batman's Hill (of course he did), a small rise of about 18 metres just south of the present-day Southern Cross Station. Surveyor Robert Hoddle used the hill as the point from which distances were measured when he laid out Melbourne's street plan the following year. The hill was gradually dug away and completely flattened between 1840 and 1892 to make way for new railway sidings and sheds. The present-day No. 2 Goods Shed, which runs along Aurora Lane and Village Street in the Docklands district, was built in 1889 on the flattened land. The Collins Street overpass, between Spencer Street and Harbour Esplanade on the south side of the station, replicates the approximate height and shape of the hill and for many years its location was also marked by a tall steel pole.

HODDLE'S GRID

The layout or 'grid' of central Melbourne's streets was designed by government surveyor Robert Hoddle in 1837. His plan, utilising the topographical survey of his predecessor, Robert Russell, rigorously followed colonial town planning regulations. However, the recently arrived Governor Bourke decided laneways should be added, primarily for better access to blocks but also for public health 'ventilation.' Rather than reduce the width of main roads to accommodate this, Hoddle simply made the blocks smaller. It is thought that streets had to be wide enough to allow for a cart with a team of horses to turn easily. Some historians also suspect that colonial authorities deliberately avoided creating a central public square or other large, open spaces to avoid crowds gathering and "a spirit of democracy breaking out."

Batman's Hill being levelled, 1840–1892. [*State Library of Victoria*]

LOCATION, LOCATION

The first sales of land in Melbourne took place in June 1837 and values rose quickly. In just four years one lucky speculator made a profit of £578 (equivalent to about $100,000 today) on a block at the corner of Elizabeth and Little Collins Streets.

GAOL TIME

The first gaol in Melbourne was a hut built on Batman's Hill in 1837. It was burnt down the following year by escaping inmates. Several temporary buildings were used until authorities constructed a new permanent prison at the top end of Russell Street, now the Old Melbourne Gaol.

SCHOOLING THE YOUNG

Batman's wife, Eliza, gave birth to seven daughters and one son, but the marriage failed and she eventually moved out. Batman then employed a governess for his children and she schooled them from a property he owned on the site of what became Prince's Bridge Hotel, now more commonly known as Young and Jackson's, on the corner of Flinders and Swanston Streets.

FIRST CHURCH

The first church building in town was the Scots' Church in Collins Street. Presbyterian services had been held on the banks of the Yarra River in 1837 and by the following year meetings were being held in a timber hut. A stone building with a 64-metre spire was completed in 1861 and for many years it was the tallest building in town. The church is now dwarfed by an office block built on church-owned land which provides rental income for the upkeep of the historic building.

MITRE 10 TAVERN

The oldest surviving building in Melbourne is believed to be the Mitre Tavern in Bank Place. It began life as a residence in 1837 and after various other uses was turned into a public house in 1868. The founders of the Mitre 10 chain of hardware stores were regulars and reputedly borrowed the name for their new enterprise. Another contender for the title of oldest is St James Old Cathedral, which was built in 1839 but dismantled and moved to its present location in King Street in 1914.

A SPIRE TO GREAT HEIGHTS

The central spire of St Paul's Cathedral in Melbourne is the highest of any Anglican (Church of England) cathedral apart from Salisbury Cathedral. St Paul's was built on the site of an earlier and much smaller parish church and, before that, a corn market. Services were held on the site from the late 1830s onwards and then the land reserved for a building in 1848. The first St Paul's Church was mostly demolished in 1885 to make way for the new cathedral which took until 1891 to construct. However, final work on the three spires did not begin until 1926. They have since become such a prominent feature of the cityscape that the original design of Federation Square had to be adjusted to avoid blocking the view of them.

ADVERTISER TO HERALD SUN

On 1 January 1838, John Pascoe Fawkner, a rival to Batman and early property speculator and entrepreneur, handwrote 32 copies of the settlement's first newspaper — the *Melbourne Advertiser*. News and advertisements were contained on one sheet of foolscap paper. He had high hopes for it, declaring "Melbourne cannot reasonably remain longer marked on the chart of advancing civilisation without its *Advertiser*." Customers could purchase a copy for a shilling or read it for free in the bar of Fawkner's own hotel. It lasted for nine editions.

Not to be deterred, he imported printing type and a wooden hand press from Tasmania and began to produce the renamed *Port Phillip Patriot and Melbourne Advertiser*. Fawkner apologised for the appearance of the first edition after the compositor he had employed failed to appear on the day and an inexperienced 18-year-old was prevailed upon to typeset the whole paper. After a further name change, to the *Daily News*, it was bought in June 1851 by the rival *The Argus*, then regarded as the city's 'paper of record.' *The Argus* published continuously until 1957 when its assets were sold to the Herald and Weekly Times company, owners of the present-day *Herald Sun*.

BOOKS PLUS

The first known bookshop in Melbourne was opened by John Fawkner in 1838 and sold mainly secondhand books — together with beer, pigs and cattle. The offerings of a rival shop that opened the following year was not limited to books either: "pit saws, fowling pieces, lady's stays, red flannel petticoats, and Epsom salts" were all available. Currently, the oldest public bookshop in Melbourne is Hill of Content in Bourke Street which opened in 1922 and sells only books and related products. Book publishing as such was slow to take off, with the first book believed to be a volume about the need to increase immigration written by the editor of the *Port Phillip Gazette*. Many early publishers were also printers or booksellers, sometimes both.

FLAG STAFFED

Erected in September 1840, the flagstaff at Flagstaff Hill was the main method of communication between the city and another flagstaff at Point Gellibrand at Williamstown. The hill was a popular place to meet and receive 'news from the bay' — and a handy location for gentlemanly pistol duels. Its use as a flag-based signal station diminished when telephany lines were strung on poles to the harbourmaster's office and the hill became, firstly, an observatory, then a cemetery and, finally, a park and gardens.

BATMAN JUNIOR

In an ironic twist of fate, in January 1845 John Batman's son, also named John, drowned while fishing near the waterfall his father had selected as the best location for the new settlement. The Yarra Falls, as they were then known, were eventually demolished in the late 1880s when Queen's Bridge was built.

BOTANIC EELS

Melbourne's Royal Botanic Gardens were founded in 1846 when an area alongside the Yarra River was reserved and four swampy lagoons that opened into the river were partially drained. The remaining lakes are home to a species of short-finned eel (*Anguilla australis*) that can grow up to 1.3 metres and — for those not already freaked out when they notice them squirming in their thousands in the water — they can slither across land when conditions are suitably moist. The eels migrate annually from the garden's lakes via drains and other watercourses and travel 4000 kilometres to the Coral Sea where they breed and die.

The Yarra Falls and bridge before the rocks were blasted away, J. H. Jones. [*State Library of Victoria*]

Newspaper poster, 1850. [*State Library of Victoria*]

2

1850–1879

Gold makes many rich
and the city booms.

VICTORIAN NAVY

From the 1850s until Federation in 1901, Victoria had its own navy. It operated from moorings at Williamstown with two warships, HMVS (Her Majesty's Victorian Ship) *Cerberus*, with a rotating gun turret, and the *Nelson*, a frigate donated by the British government, plus gunboats *Victoria* and *Albert*, and some smaller torpedo boats. Crews and shore staff were a mixture of full-time and volunteer men. The ships became part of the Commonwealth Naval Forces upon Federation and, later, helped form the new Royal Australian Navy. Volunteers also formed Melbourne's only land defence force after British troops withdrew

HMVS Cerberus in 1871. [*State Library of Victoria*]

The second Prince's Bridge, also known as Lennox Bridge, J. G. Boyd, c.1849. [*State Library of Victoria*]

from the colony in 1870 until a regular, paid militia was constituted in 1884.

PRINCES BRIDGES

The site of the present-day Princes Bridge was already a popular crossing spot, with punts ferrying locals across the river for a fee, when a simple wooden trestle toll bridge known as Balbirnies Bridge was built in 1843. Later, in November 1850, came the narrow, single-arched bluestone and granite structure you see in this illustration. It was known as Lennox Bridge after its designer until renamed in honour of Prince Albert, Queen Victoria's consort. At the time it was the longest stone-arch bridge built anywhere in Australia. Today's much wider Princes Bridge was not constructed until 1888.

GOLD FEVER

On the discovery of gold, 50 of the 55 members of the Melbourne City Police resigned on the same day in 1851 and left for the goldfields to seek their fortune. Excitement about gold drew thousands more to the increasingly wealthy city. According to the most reliable estimates, between 1851 and 1861 the population of the city area grew from 29,000 to 125,000, a surge that put serious pressure on city infrastructure and created significant problems with sanitation, public health and crime. But gold also meant that huge amounts of money flowed into town and many substantial public and commercial buildings were constructed. Many 'diggers' became extremely wealthy and gold became the mainstay of the local economy, surpassing agricultural products, particularly wool.

Cricket match between Australia and England, 1876. [*State Library of Victoria*]

MOVING A GROUND

The Melbourne Cricket Ground (MCG) moved to its present site, on land previously known as Government or Police Paddock in 1853. Until then it had been used as a staging area for colonial troopers and barracks for mounted police. Before that, the site is believed to have been an Aboriginal camping ground. The MCG is home to the Melbourne Cricket Club which played its first game on the site of the Old Mint in William Street before moving to four other locations, eventually settling at the Police Paddock site, mainly because it sloped enough to avoid flooding.

CHIEF OF NOBODY

Why does Victoria have a Chief Commissioner of police when there are no other Commissioners to be Chief of? I'm glad you asked. Apart from the City Police, there were once six other autonomous police forces in the Colony, each with its own commanding officer. These forces included the Native Police Corps (a joint venture between settlers and local Aboriginals), and the Water Police stationed at Williamstown. In 1853 all such forces were combined to form Victoria Police under a single *Chief* Commissioner — but although the other Commissioner roles faded away, the title of Chief remains to this day.

Fake 'Digger Wedding,' 1853, S. T. Gill. [*State Library of Victoria*]

INSTITUTIONS ESTABLISHED

The foundation stones of both the University of Melbourne and the State Library, then called the Melbourne Public Library, were laid on the same day, 3 July 1854, by Governor Charles Hotham. The creation of both institutions had been championed by Supreme Court Judge Redmond Barry whose statue now stands in front of the Library. He became the first Chancellor of the University and President of the Trustees of the Library. The first four professors of the University each received £1000 and a rent-free house for life. One of them, Fredrick McCoy, Professor of Natural History, did not have a university degree but had somehow managed to become a senior dean at Queen's

College, Belfast. The total annual endowment for the University was set at £9,000, equivalent to approximately $900,000 today.

FAKE DIGGER WEDDINGS

Successful 'diggers' returning to Melbourne from the goldfields found creative ways to flaunt their new and almost obscene levels of wealth. One was to hire an expensive, open-topped, horse-drawn carriage with pretty young women and pretend to be part of an opulent wedding party. Fake Digger Weddings became all the rage and diggers would compete to see who could be the biggest peacock.

STEAMED BISCUITS

Thomas Swallow founded Australia's first biscuit making factory using steam-driven machinery in Sandridge, now Port Melbourne, in 1854. Swallow arrived in Australia from England via California and Ballarat where he had made a considerable profit selling Colt revolvers. He took on a partner and, as the Swallow & Ariell Steam Biscuit Company, expanded into other products. The company supplied ships as well as shops and they were the first to introduce 'fancy' biscuits. They also made cakes and ice cream, Marie biscuits and Melba wafers. The ice cream business

Railway Pier (now Station Pier) in Sandridge, (now Port Melbourne), c.1875. [State Library of Victoria]

was sold to Peters Ice Cream in 1958 and, after a period of consolidation in the industry, the biscuit division ended up as part of the Australian Biscuit Company, which was later rebranded Arnott's. The original factory building in Stokes Street, Port Melbourne is now heritage-listed.

FIRST RAILWAY

Station Pier in Port Melbourne, where nowadays enormous international cruise ships dock and disgorge their passengers for day trips, was initially called Railway Pier and the area was known as Sandridge. In 1854 the pier boasted the first railway line in Australia, with track running the length of the pier and then three miles into the city centre where it terminated at what later became Flinders Street Station.

EXHIBITIONARY

There have been three Exhibition Buildings in Melbourne. The first was a predominantly glass structure, erected in haste for the Great Exhibition of 1854, and designed to resemble the huge 'Crystal Palace' built in London for the British Great Exhibition a few years earlier. It was also meant to be a prelude to another international event — the Paris *Exposition Universelle* — being held in 1855. As a gimmick, the first edition of *The Age* newspaper was printed on a state-of-the-art steam-driven press at the exhibition.

A second Exhibition Hall was constructed in 1866 at the site of what is now the State Library La Trobe Reading Room, before the present Exhibition Buildings were completed in 1880. As can be seen in the illustration overleaf, the complex featured an array of additional wings and some shedding. After World War II British migrants were temporarily housed in rows of huts at the rear of the building. The Royal prefix was granted by Queen Elizabeth II and officially added to the name of the building in 1980.

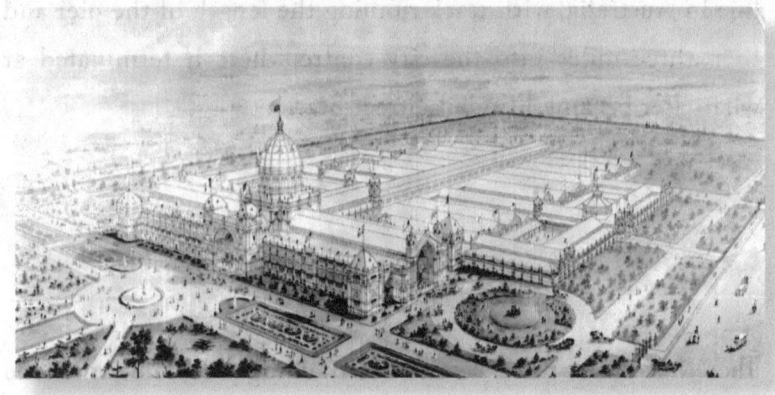

The Exhibition Buildings, completed in 1880, showing the extensive annexes. [*State Library of Victoria*]

GUN SLOTS

Construction of Parliament House in Spring Street began in 1855 and, arguably, because it does not yet have its dome as originally designed, has not yet been completed. This did not stop artists of the day doing some wishful thinking and adding the dome to drawings and paintings. It was built in stages, with the Legislative Assembly and Legislative Council chambers opening for business on 25 November 1856. Other parts of the building were gradually added and completed by 1929.

The building has a spiral staircase leading to a marksman's position, gun slots, a prison cell and a 'secret' tunnel leading to a bilge room (and not the Imperial Hotel across the street as widely rumoured). The defensive elements were added after an attack on the building in August 1860 by 3000 rioters demanding land reform. The building served as the Federal Parliament building after Federation in 1901 until completion of Parliament House in Canberra in 1926.

STATE LIBRARY

Melbourne Public Library, now the State Library of Victoria, opened in 1856 with 3846 books. Today it contains approximately four million items, including books, newspapers, sound recordings, pictures, and maps. The oldest individual written item is a Cuneiform tablet, dating from *c.*2050 BC and the oldest book is *Boethius' De musica*, a late 10th-century manuscript. A raised wooden platform in the centre of the domed La Trobe Reading Room was once used by librarians to 'shoosh' patrons who disturbed others. When the room was refurbished in the early 2000s, the contractors were able to trace the suppliers of the original floor covering — a firm in Glasgow — and order exactly the same kind of linoleum.

TAKING A PUNT

If you believe, as many do, that the busy and congested thoroughfare Punt Road was named after the gambling 'punts' taken by spectators at sports events or the hand 'punting' of the ball in Australian Rules football, you would be wrong. It actually refers

Punt Road Yarra River crossing 1856, looking south from the Richmond side. [*State Library of Victoria*]

to the punt once used to ferry people across the Yarra River at that spot. The bridge carrying Punt Road over the river was not completed until 1938.

SECRET ELECTIONS

Victoria became the first jurisdiction anywhere in the world to organise parliamentary elections on the basis of a secret ballot. After much vitriolic debate and general argy-bargy, during which even the colony's Attorney-General angrily denounced secret ballots as "un-English" and "unconstitutional," a system of printed ballot papers was devised and elections were held between August and October 1856.

BARRACKING

The oldest part of the Victoria Barracks complex in St Kilda Road was built between 1856 and 1858 by the same regiment of British troops that had helped to suppress the Eureka uprising. The barracks became the base for Victoria's own defence forces before becoming the headquarters of the new Australian Department of Defence after Federation. During World War II the barracks housed the Australian War Cabinet and the Australian forces Commander-in-Chief, Sir Thomas Blamey, but not, as widely believed, Supreme Commander of Allied Forces in the South-West Pacific Area General Douglas MacArthur, who camped out at the swanky Menzies Hotel and used empty offices in Collins Street as his official headquarters.

PRISON BOSS BASHED

In 1857, John Price, Inspector-General of Victoria's penal establishments, was bashed to death by inmates housed on hulks (decommissioned ships) being used to manage an overflow of convicts. The inmates were aggrieved about worsening living conditions and inadequate food rations and the Inspector-General agreed to meet them to hear their complaints. At a well-timed moment, several men grabbed an unarmed Price, knocked him down, and battered him with stones and rocks. Convicts who escaped during the melee were later recaptured and seven perpetrators were hanged.

GAS LIT

By 1857, gas had become readily available for street lighting. Lamps were lit 30 minutes after sunset and kept alight until dawn. Although they were eventually replaced by electric street lighting, authorities could not be bothered to completely remove all the gas lamp posts and they were often cut off at waist height and capped. Looking like bollards, some of them remain on Melbourne streets today, usually painted green or white.

Cut-down gas lamp on the corner of Rathdown and Barkley Streets in Carlton.

POOLED RESOURCES

In early Melbourne, few homes had proper washing facilities and city residents would wash in any open water they could find. In 1860, fearful of an epidemic of typhoid as the result of residents bathing in polluted rivers, the city council opened the City Baths in Swanston Street. For men there were individual bath tubs, a swimming pool, and a gymnasium. Women had separate baths and a swimming pool. There were also Turkish steam baths, a Jewish ceremonial bath and a laundry. Maintaining the social class system of the era, there were second-class facilities in the basement with first-class on the level above. The complex became dilapidated and was re-built in 1904.

DOING THE BLOCK

For seven decades, from the 1860s to the 1930s, if you wanted to be considered a member of the trendy Melbourne social scene — a *fashionista* we might say today — the place to *be* was along a particular section of Collins Street at certain times of the week. From 3.30 pm to 5.30 pm on weekdays and between 11 am and 2 pm on Saturdays, Melburnians could put on their finest clobber and parade along the block of Collins Street between Elizabeth and Swanston Streets, pretending to window shop but actually eyeing up others equally keen to be noticed. Several shops burnt down in 1889 and a new shopping arcade arose in their place.

It took its name from the ritual, becoming The Block Arcade. The Gill drawing on page xiii illustrates 'Doing the Block' in the 1860s and the photograph opposite shows the scene in 1911. While many thought of it as a kind of side-show, in 1919 *The Argus* declared that "to those who are drawn to it by the grey magnet of its pavement, it is the centre of all things, it is Melbourne incarnate — in a word it is 'the Block'."

BODIES AND BLOOD

One of the first morgues to be built in Melbourne was erected at Williamstown in 1860. It was constructed at the water's edge to allow the tides to wash away blood and bodily waste after inquests. Corpses were hung from the ceiling so rats would not be able to get at them. The building was relocated at least twice and now forms part of the Seaworks Maritime Precinct in Williamstown.

WIN, BUT NO CUP

The first Melbourne Cup race in 1861 was won by Archer in the slowest time ever recorded (but equalled by Lantern in 1864). Archer's actual owners received zilch because at the time the horse was leased to its trainer, Etienne de Mestre, who received

Doing The Block c.1911. [*State Library of Victoria*]

a hand-beaten gold watch and a cheque for 710 gold sovereigns, but not a cup. The first time an actual trophy was presented at the race was in 1865. But it still wasn't a cup. Instead, the owner of the winning horse was given a fancy silver bowl imported from England — which he considered so ugly that he sold it shortly after. It was not until 1915 that a gold cup as we know it today was designed and manufactured locally and presented to the winner. For several years the winning jockey was also given a gold whip (see page 52). No horse starting from barrier 18 has ever won the race, and barrier 5 has been the most successful. Horses with the numbers 4 and 12 have had the most wins, with 11 each. For the first few years, the race was run on a Thursday, not the now-traditional Tuesday.

DRAMATIC UPS AND DOWNS

In 1861, at the age of 42 years, and soon after his wife had died, distinguished actor and Melbourne theatre impresario, George Coppin, married his 18-year-old stepdaughter who was already three months pregnant. Coppin had a rollercoaster career, becoming wealthy and going bust several times over. He also became a member of the state parliament while still running his theatre empire. He is best remembered for establishing the Cremorne Gardens Amusement Park and owning, then losing, but eventually saving the Theatre Royal in Bourke Street.

MONUMENTAL ROUNDABOUT

Among the many street hazards during the late 1800s were monuments and statues plonked in the middle of the road. From 1865 a stone monument to explorers Burke and Wills stood bang in the middle of the junction of Collins and Russell Streets, opposite the Scots' Church, facing down Collins Street. It was moved to Spring Street in 1886, then Swanston Street in 1890, and then taken into storage because of underground railway construction works in 2017. Another, less obtrusive, monument to the same explorers stands in Royal Park and marks the actual point of departure of their expedition.

DETECTIVE ADDICT

The longest serving member of the early Melbourne detective force was Fook Shing, a Chinese-Australian whose heroin and gambling addictions were well known but deliberately overlooked by senior officers. For 20 years until 1886, he was their 'insider' and guide to the thriving Chinese community in and around Little Bourke Street, acting as interpreter and investigating crime there and in rural areas with large Chinese populations. Shing arrived in the 1850s as part of a wave of Chinese immigration during the gold rush and settled at Bendigo where he became the 'headman' or 'Chief of the Chinese' before moving to the city. His addictions were often subsidised by his superiors who saw it as a necessary evil in order to obtain information about criminals who ran gambling dens in the laneways of Chinatown.

Portrait of Fook Shing in the British *Graphic* magazine in 1880.

UNCIVIL THREAT

In February 1865, a Confederate States Navy warship unexpectedly arrived and anchored in Hobsons Bay. The captain reputedly threatened to fire on Melbourne unless it was allowed to replenish supplies and finish repairs. Reluctantly, the authorities acquiesced. After staying for almost a month, and illegally recruiting replacement crew, the CSS *Shenandoah* resumed its mission of disrupting supplies bound for the Union side during the American Civil War. An international tribunal in 1872 found Victoria and, by default, the British government, responsible for all acts of aggression by the *Shenandoah* after it left Melbourne.

LIFTING THE CITY

The first hydraulic lift (or elevator) in a building in Melbourne was installed in 1865. It was intended for goods rather than people and it was not until the 1880s that the first dedicated passenger lifts started to appear. Their introduction enabled buildings to be built to greater heights, with the Australia Building on the corner of Elizabeth Street and Flinders Lane able to get to a record-breaking 12 floors. It remained the tallest commercial building in Melbourne for four decades. The Exhibition Building in Carlton even installed one of the new-fangled lifts during Centennial celebrations in 1888, enabling visitors to reach the dome's viewing platform comfortably.

SMELLY LILY

At three metres wide, the giant water lily *Victoria amazonica* in Melbourne's Royal Botanic Gardens blooms for just 48 hours — and thousands come to see and smell it. Discovered in the Bolivian rainforest in 1801 and brought to the Gardens by the first director, Baron Ferdinand von Mueller, there were doubts it would survive, but in 1867 it flowered for the first time, drawing hundreds to see it and experience the pleasant butterscotch and pineapple scent. On the other hand, another 'big flower' at the gardens, the *titan arum* lily (*Amorphophallus titanum*) from Sumatra, is said to smell like a 'dead possum' and opens for just three days before collapsing into a boggy heap.

THE TIVOLI

The Melbourne Opera House opened in Bourke Street, close to the junction with Swanston Street, in August 1872 and for the next three decades presented a range of mostly light opera, burlesque and vaudeville shows. It was also the venue of the first showing of a motion picture in Australia in 1895. After being closed down by the health department and rebuilt in 1901 as the New Opera House it became famous for music hall and vaudeville entertainments. International performers who appeared included Marie Lloyd, W. C. Fields, and the famous illusionist Houdini. It was renamed the Tivoli Theatre in 1912 and then became a cinema before being destroyed by fire in 1967. The site then became a shopping arcade and has most recently been redeveloped as an RMIT University building.

MAKE A LAKE

Albert Park Lake was formed from lagoons in the swampy 'delta' between Emerald Hill (now South Melbourne) and Port Phillip Bay. The lagoons were gradually drained between 1873 and 1890 with the silt used as infill to form a permanent lake, and named for Queen Victoria's husband Prince Albert. Fresh water from the Yarra River was diverted to fill the lake. The area around it was initially used as a racing track for horses and buggies and a speedway opened in 1903. The park is known internationally as the site of the annual Formula 1 Grand Prix motor race with barriers and stands being erected around its roads.

Another swamp, Sandridge Lagoon, reaching inland from the Bay to present-day Raglan Street, was not completely filled in until the 1920s when the area around the boat harbour below Rouse Street was finally reclaimed. Residents had long complained about the smell and poisonous water but it was subject to political buck-passing until the Port Melbourne Lagoon Act was passed in 1889. Factories and houses were built on the reclaimed land and a public park, cleverly called Lagoon Reserve, established on part of it.

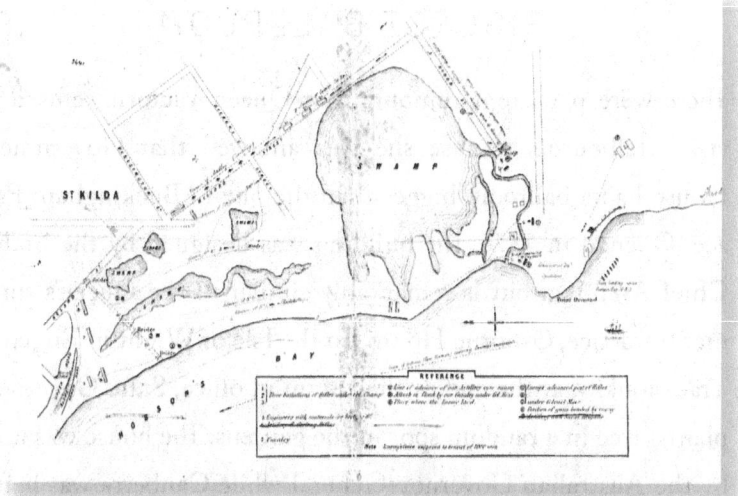

Map produced for a military exercise around Elwood in 1862 showing swamps in the area. [*State Library of Victoria*]

CHEAP EATS

In 1870s Melbourne, breakfast or dinner could be bought for a mere sixpence from one of the many cafes that sprang up to satisfy the burgeoning population. For your money (approximately $4 today) you could get a breakfast with a choice of ten meat dishes, bread and butter, and tea or coffee. For dinner there would be soups, pies and meat dishes such as boiled mutton or corned beef, and puddings. For a night out, if you were prepared to double your money to a shilling (around $9), you could also have alcohol.

BIGGEST BALLROOM

There were persistent rumours that Queen Victoria refused to visit Melbourne because she was annoyed that Government House had a ballroom bigger than the one in Buckingham Palace. Opened in 1876, the building was designed by the State's Chief Architect but is remarkably similar to the Queen's summer residence, Osborne House, on the Isle of Wight in England. Traditionally, at the end of their term in office, State Governors plant a tree in a random spot in the gardens. The house was used by the Australian Governor-General while Canberra was being built and the Victorian Governor temporarily relocated to 'Stonnington,' a large house in Malvern.

ENTERTAINMENT WIRTH

The site of the present-day Arts Centre in St Kilda Road has long been an area where the masses went for entertainment. American touring circus Cooper and Bailey — one of many to visit Melbourne — first pitched their marquee on the site in 1877. The same block of land was later leased by the FitzGerald family who built a permanent circus building called Olympia. Close by, in an area known as Princes Court, there was a Japanese tea house, a café, a wine bar, a rifle range, the death-defying Camel Back Toboggan, and the Canadian Water Chute. The

Outside Wirth's Circus in St Kilda Road, 1945. [*State Library of Victoria*]

Wirth circus family took over the entire Olympia site in 1907 and added a roller-skating rink and a cinema. It remained hugely popular until 1953 when 'Wirth's Park' burnt down and the site became a car park.

READY TO GO

According to the official police regulations of 1877, Melbourne officers were to remain in their uniform at *all* times. It could be removed to sleep, but even then it had to be kept close by in case of an urgent call-out. The uniform itself was an exact copy of the one worn by the London Metropolitan Police, including the famous 'chimney' hat that allowed constables to be seen from afar and, in theory, deter criminal activity in their designated area or 'Beat.' Based on city blocks, the Beat was to be patrolled at a steady walking pace of two miles an hour and constables were subject to frequent surprise inspections by supervisors.

MARKET BODIES

The popular Queen Victoria Market opened in 1878, after evolving gradually from a meat market established close by in 1868. The sheds and car park for the market are partly built on the Old Melbourne Cemetery which operated from 1837 to 1854. Several hundred bodies were relocated to Fawkner Cemetery at the time but it has been estimated something like 9000 corpses are still buried, mostly under the car park. Melbourne City Council has undertaken to exhume and re-bury bodies when the market area is redeveloped.

The 'Queen Vic' is the last survivor of three major markets established in Melbourne during the late 1800s, the others being the Eastern Market on the corner of Bourke and Exhibition Streets (demolished 1960) and the Western Market between Collins and William Streets (demolished 1961). There were also other specialised markets selling fruit and vegetables, fish and meat, and hay and corn.

A busy Saturday morning at the Queen Victoria Market in 1879. [*State Library of Victoria*]

NOT JUST CRICKET

The Melbourne Cricket Club (MCC) began building courts for the exciting new game of 'Lawn Tennis' in 1879 and organised the first state championships a year later. The game had arrived in Australia not long before, via boxed sets of the required paraphernalia produced by the game's inventor, a certain Major Walter Wingfield, who had wanted to call it SPHAIRISTIKE. The MCC also initiated national tennis championships when they invited the Sydney Cricket Club to an interstate competition in 1905. Apart from tennis, the MCC has been actively involved in many other sports, including Australian Rules Football, hockey, lacrosse, and croquet. Management of the Melbourne Cricket Ground is currently delegated to the MCC by the state government. The club itself has been described as the most exclusive in Australia, and it can take more than 30 years on a waiting list to be granted full membership,

The front of Parliament House, Spring Street, Melbourne, under construction, 1880. [*State Library of Victoria*]

3

1880–1899

The people are entertained
but things soon go bust.

KELLY SAYINGS

The words "Such is life" spoken by Ned Kelly as he was about to be hanged in Old Melbourne Gaol in November 1880 are widely known, but such pithy expressions were clearly a habit of the Kelly family. His mother, Ellen, a prisoner in the same gaol at the time, is said to have visited him in his cell the night before the execution and exhorted him "Mind you die like a Kelly, son."

WILLIAM'S CREEK

Elizabeth Street follows the route of an old watercourse called William's Creek and was prone to major flooding for decades. Some early sketches of the city even show the street with ramps and small bridges across it. The situation did not ease until

William's Creek outfall on the north bank of the Yarra.

the 1880s, when underground stormwater drains were built throughout the city. In 1883 William's Creek was diverted into a large pipe, which still runs the length of Elizabeth Street, goes under Flinders Street Station and disgorges into the Yarra River just a few metres to the east of the pedestrian bridge linking the station with Southbank.

LOUD BANDING

During the 1880s, some Melbourne city residents became so annoyed by the constant street-preaching and marching of the newly-established evangelical Salvation Army with their loud brass bands that they formed a rival 'Skeleton Army.' Members wore cross-and-bones caps and strode alongside the marchers in drunken attempts to cause trouble. The Salvationists were pelted with stones and eggs and sharp objects and sometimes physically attacked and injured.

On the other hand, members of the Army occasionally let their enthusiasm get the better of them. Captain William Shepherd was hauled before the District Court in April 1883 because he had not obtained the necessary permit for marching. He was fined £5 plus costs for "causing annoyance and defying the laws" with the bench hoping it would be a warning to the Salvation Army generally. The Salvos later gained wide community respect and support for their welfare work among the poor and vulnerable.

BUNNY BONNETS

The first felt hat factory in Australia was founded in Melbourne in the early 1880s. Using rabbit fur as the main ingredient, production was subject to a range of hazardous processes to shape and smooth the felt. Some of these involved using dangerous chemicals which, naturally enough, led to serious health problems among workers. One such illness, the so-called 'mad hatters' disease, was essentially mercury poisoning of the central nervous system.

The Denton hat factory in Collingwood, 1882. [*State Library of Victoria*]

BARRY AND BARROW

Sir Redmond Barry, a respectable and upstanding Melbourne establishment figure, had a long-term mistress, Louise Barrow, with whom he had four children. Sir Redmond was responsible for helping to establish major Melbourne institutions (Melbourne Public Library, the University of Melbourne) and, as a Supreme Court judge, presided over major trials (Eureka rebellion, Ned Kelly). He did not marry Louise, possibly because he was a Protestant and she a Catholic. Nevertheless, he supported their children and bought her a house. They are buried alongside each other in the Melbourne General Cemetery.

CLOCKING ON AND OFF

Quickly becoming a Melbourne landmark, the so-called Water Tower Clock was initially installed in 1883 at the Elizabeth Street entrance to Flinders Street Station (see overleaf). After a visit to Princes Bridge Station while Flinders Street was being rebuilt, it moved to Spencer Street Station in 1910 where it remained until 1967. It then 'disappeared' into private hands for a while but was bought by the state government and restored with a new electronic mechanism. After being displayed at the Scienceworks museum in Spotswood the clock was re-erected in 2014 on top of a lurid electronic advertising screen back at Southern Cross Station (the old Spencer Street).

A cable car passing the Water Clock Tower at the Elizabeth Street entrance of Flinders Street Station, 1900. [*State Library of Victoria*]

HOME TO CHLOÉ

Chloé, the famous painting of a young, nude model now hanging in Young and Jackson's Hotel, was bought in 1883 by Dr Thomas Fitzgerald after it had been exhibited in Paris, Sydney and Melbourne. He subsequently loaned the painting to the National Gallery of Victoria (NGV), but removed it from view when there was an outcry about it being displayed on Sundays. On Fitzgerald's death in 1908 it was bought by the owner of Young and Jackson's where it has hung ever since, apart from a brief return visit to the NGV in 1995.

Many soldiers who drank at the hotel and who went on to fight in various wars and conflicts wrote to Chloé expressing their heartfelt admiration for her and promising to return. Such was

Chloé's popularity that in 1909, Melbourne's *Punch* magazine published a poem referring to "Chloé the chaste. With the good Greek waist."

A GRAND NAME

When the Windsor Hotel, in Spring Street, was built in 1884 it was known simply as The Grand. Bought in 1886 by James Munro, a leader of the Melbourne temperance movement, it was renamed The Grand Coffee Palace and the owner ceremoniously burnt the hotel's liquor licence. He also added the ballroom, a sweeping staircase and turrets from which guests were able to see the You Yang hills in one direction and the Dandenong Ranges in the other. It was sold again in 1897, expanded and relicensed, and the name changed back to the Grand Hotel. It changed hands yet again in 1920 and after another major refurbishment the new owner changed the name to the Windsor Hotel following the visit of Prince Edward, the British Prince of Wales.

After several more owners, including for a short time the Victorian state government, and having survived several controversial attempts at redevelopment, the hotel was bought by the wealthy Halim family of Indonesia. The building remains the only surviving example of a Victorian-era Renaissance Revival-style hotel in Melbourne and is currently branded simply as 'The Windsor.'

Dignitaries at Melbourne Zoo in 1895. [*Public Record Office Victoria*]

ZOO CONTROL

During the 1880s, the Zoo in Parkville became such a hugely popular venue for families that on Sundays, when there was no admission fee, police officers had to be assigned to guard the entrances and provide crowd control because of the large numbers trying to enter.

THE ROYAL MAIL HOTEL

The Royal Mail Hotel, which stood on the south-east corner of Bourke and Swanston Streets, was once the venue for the annual presentation of a gold whip to the winning jockey of that day's Melbourne Cup race. Bought in 1848 by Edward Green, a former British army officer, with profits from his Melbourne to New South Wales mail and stagecoach run, the Royal Mail was later sold to William Sugden, who had to resign as Chief Constable in order to take over the licence, but kept his job of chief of the fire brigade. Being so centrally located, the hotel quickly became the base for horse-drawn cabs in the city, with many of them lined up along the centre of Swanston Street while waiting for passengers.

By 1888, when the annual tradition of the gold whip began, the hotel had obtained a rare licence allowing it to remain open after 9 pm. The hotel was demolished in 1960 and a nondescript multi-storey office block now stands in its place. It can be recognised as the building with the full-length, electronic advertising panel facing Bourke Street Mall.

The Royal Mail Hotel in 1938. [*State Library of Victoria*]

MARVELLOUS SMELLBOOM

The familiar term 'Marvellous Melbourne' can be traced to a series of articles in the London *Daily Telegraph* in 1885. Visiting the city, journalist George Augustus Sala was impressed by "handsome shops ... crowded with bustling well-dressed people," and declared Melbourne to be "magnificent and marvellous." However, according to one historian, while many locals expressed delight in this positive view of their hometown, others suggested similar but less favourable descriptions, such as 'Marvellous Smellboom' and 'Murderous Melbourne.'

HORSES TO CABLE CARS

Inspired by the new cable car system in San Francisco, Francis Clapp bought the local patents and started the Melbourne Tramway Company. Clapp owned one of the horse-drawn Cobb & Co routes from Melbourne to Ballarat and had already successfully operated several horse-drawn tramways throughout the city, undercutting cabs, and seeing off a rival. The first cable car ran in November 1885 from the junction of Spencer and Bourke Streets, along Flinders Street to Richmond and Hawthorn. Other routes followed, and the Melbourne cable car system, which required heavy underground cables to pull carriages, grew to approximately 75 kilometres of track before being fully replaced by electric trams in November 1940. The powerhouse for the Nicholson Street Line cable remains at the corner of Nicholson and Gertrude Streets, Fitzroy.

AIRFIELD ON THE SWAMP

Coode Island, between Docklands and Yarraville, was formed in 1886 when engineer Sir John Coode was commissioned to create a channel cutting off a loop of the Yarra River and thus shortening the distance to the Bay by 3.5 kilometres. When the canal was finished, the western section of the loop of the Yarra became the beginning of the Maribyrnong River, while the rest

Coode Island fire, 1991.

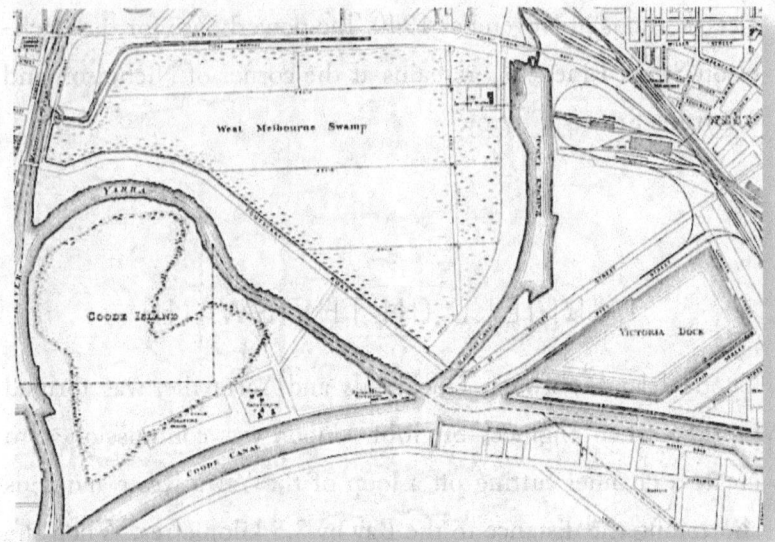

Extract from a 1910 Department of Lands and Surveys map showing the old course of the Yarra and the new Coode Canal shortcut. [*State Library of Victoria*]

gradually silted up to the point it was longer strictly an 'island.' The surrounding area was generally known as the West Melbourne Swamp and used variously as an animal quarantine station, a sanatorium for bubonic plague sufferers, and a home to hermits who lived in shacks and abandoned boats and scavenged the many rubbish dumps. It later became the site of an aircraft factory and aerodrome and has been used for storing petrochemicals since the 1960s.

Some of the storage tanks caught fire in August 1991 and Melbourne was blanketed with toxic smoke and fumes for two days. Despite being extinguished on the first day, the tanks reignited the following day.

HOME TOWN GIRL

In 1887, operatic soprano Dame Nellie Melba — who was born in the inner suburb of Richmond and took her stage name from her native city — signed a 10 year contract for 1000 francs per year with the impresario Maurice Strakosch. Almost immediately she received a much better offer of 3000 francs per *month* from an opera house in Brussels. To her dismay Strakosch refused to release her from their contract but matters were resolved when he died suddenly a short time afterwards. Nellie made her operatic debut at La Monnaie in Brussels four days later. So widespread was her reputation that she was invited to sing in the world's first ever radio concert, broadcast in England in 1920 from a disused packing shed used as a studio by the Marconi company.

Nellie's birth name was Helen Porter Mitchell and her father, businessman and builder, David Mitchell, built the Exhibition Buildings in Carlton, the Scots' Church in Collins Street, and other notable buildings in the city. She was so popular that a number of food items were named after her, including Melba Toast, Melba Wafers, a chicken and truffles dish called Melba Garniture, and Peach Melba, first made for her at the prestigious Savoy Hotel in London. In more recent years a highway, a road tunnel and a retirement village have been given her name. Nellie announced her retirement from singing in 1926 but it was two years before she gave her final performance, giving rise to the phrase 'doing a Melba,' referring to an extended departure. Dame Nellie died in 1931.

UNIQUELY ROYAL

RMIT University began life as the Working Men's College in 1887 to provide an educational facility for the 'working people' of Melbourne. It was funded jointly by grazier and educational philanthropist Francis Ormond and the Trade Hall Council and added the 'Royal' prefix in 1954 after permission was granted by Queen Elizabeth II. It became the Royal Melbourne Institute of Technology in 1960 and then RMIT University in 1992. It remains the only higher education institution in Australia authorised to use the 'Royal' prefix.

ORANGES AND BANANAS

In December 1888, citizens of Melbourne were greatly alarmed by the number of actual and potential accidents being caused by orange and banana peel thrown casually to the ground. A writer to *The Argus* noted that a friend had recently sustained life-threatening injuries and he himself had witnessed an elderly gentleman narrowly avoid a severe fall. *The Argus* editor pointed out that banana skins, particularly in Swanston Street, seemed to be more dangerous than orange peel and recommended that street 'sweepers,' mostly children employed to remove horse manure before it became dry and dusty, be instructed to pay special attention to the growing menace.

THEATRE GHOST

Melbourne's most famous theatre ghost is Frederick Federici, who suffered a heart attack while being lowered from the stage into the basement of the Princess's [sic] Theatre during an opera in 1888. There have been many sightings of his ghost over the years and it became a tradition to leave an empty seat in the third row on opening nights so he wouldn't roam around during performances and distract cast members. He has also lent his name to a restaurant at the front of the theatre. Another famous Melbourne ghost is that of a fisherman who drowned close to Flinders Street Station and is said to float around platform 10 in the middle of the night.

NOT 1888, NOT REALLY

The iconic and grand '1888 Building' at the University of Melbourne wasn't built in 1888, nor was it actually part of the University when it was constructed. While the land facing Gratton Street *was* initially owned by the University, it was sold off to the State Public Works Department. Building then took place in three stages between 1889 and 1892 for what was, firstly, a teacher training college and then a hostel for students at the nearby University High School. The site finally returned to full University ownership in 1989 and is now the Graduate Centre.

COFFEE CULTURE

On its completion in 1888, the Federal Coffee Palace hotel on the corner of King and Collins Streets was the largest hotel in Australia. It had 370 bedrooms and was built by leading members of the temperance movement to encourage people away from consumption of alcohol. The ornately designed hotel became a tourist attraction in its own right and produced a guide to other coffee palaces such the Grand and the Victoria. Coffee has remained a significant feature of Melbourne culture, particularly as a result of Italian immigration during the 1950s, and locally trained baristas are much sought after internationally. It has been estimated that three million cups are bought each day in the city and surrounding suburbs.

BURIED TREASURE

In July 1889, 3712 gold sovereigns were discovered hidden under the platform of Williamstown Railway Station. The coins were found by two curious young boys who had noticed a mouse disappear into a hole under the platform. The coins had been stolen a few months earlier from the cargo ship *Iberia* which had been loaded with bags containing a total of 5000 sovereigns as she lay at the end of the Williamstown Railway Pier. Naturally, when local residents heard of the find, they attempted to locate

The East Melbourne Cyclorama in 1889. [*State Library of Victoria*]

the balance of the haul, presenting problems for police officers who were forced to keep guard at the station. The missing coins were never found ... as far as we know.

THE CYCLORAMAS

Before cinemas, there were the Cycloramas — windowless, hexagonal buildings to which spectators flocked between 1889 and 1906. Patrons would enter the one in Victoria Street, East Melbourne, through a turnstile and ascend a stairway to a central platform (the 'Mound') from where they could view scenes of an historical event all around them, painted on the internal wall, together with 3D models of objects and participants in the event. The first presentation described the famous Battle of Waterloo. There was another Cyclorama in Little Collins Street that opened with 'The Siege of Paris.'

FLASH LITTLE LON

In 1889, city police officers claimed they knew of 17 separate brothels operating in the area bounded by Spring, Little Bourke, Exhibition (previously Stephen) and Lonsdale Streets, known colloquially as 'Little Lon.' The upmarket 'Flash Houses' were located along Lonsdale Street, many of them operated by 'Madam Brussels,' whose real name was the more mundane Caroline Hodgson. It was claimed that her high-class clientele (rumoured to include judges and politicians) protected her from prosecution and, of course, it may have helped that her husband was a policeman.

BABY BLUES

In October 1889, the Grand National Baby Show being held at the Exhibition Buildings ended in a near-riot when the organiser was accused of being related to the winning child. According to *The Age*, the building was packed with "hundreds of rosy little cherubim ... served up by their attendants in the most delectable manner like oysters on the shell." But when the time came to award the Champion Baby prize to Florence Johnston of East Melbourne, a voice called out from the audience that she was the niece of Alfred Dampier, the theatre entrepreneur who had arranged the event. This was later found to be false but it did not stop a "scene of considerable disorder, in which there were all sorts of cries of dissatisfaction" with stalls and tables being overturned. Police were called to restore order and the winning baby and her mother were finally escorted from the building.

THE NINE-BY-FIVE EXHIBITION

In 1889, a small group of artists held an exhibition in a gallery in Swanston Street in which most of the 183 works were painted on the lids of wooden cigar boxes, approximately nine by five inches (23 cms x 12.5 cms). The group, Charles Conder, Tom Roberts and Arthur Streeton, are now more famously known as founding members of the Heidelberg School of Australian impressionist art. The works sold for between one and nine guineas each and one art critic declared that most of them were "a pain to the eye." Roberts' *By The Treasury* was bought by the National Gallery of Victoria in 2002 for $200,000 and a collection of four works valued at $3 million was donated to the Art Gallery of South Australia in 2012.

LIFE EXPECTANCY

The average life expectancy of a boy born in Melbourne in 1890 was 51.1 years and for girls 54.8 years. For comparison, a boy born in 2022 could expect to live to 81.2 years and a girl to 85.3 years.

RIPPER SPECULATION

A man arrested for a brutal murder in Melbourne in 1891 is believed by some 'experts' to have been the infamous London serial killer Jack the Ripper. When local detectives investigated Fredrick Bayley Deeming's background they discovered he had spent a lifetime roaming the world, having lived in Britain, South Africa, Uruguay, and several states in Australia. He had used different names, married at least twice, and been involved in a number of frauds and robberies. He was also wanted in England for the murder of his first wife and their four children. While on the run, Deeming married Emily Mather and in December 1881 they travelled to Melbourne where he murdered her and hid her body under a fireplace.

As news spread, considerable speculation arose in Britain and Australia about his possible role in the Whitechapel murders. Piecing together his timeline, some 'Ripperologists' believe that Deeming was in England on the appropriate dates but, as with

A 1892 newspaper illustration suggesting a similarity between Fredrick Deeming and 'Jack the Viper,' one of the alternative names for the Whitechapel serial killer. [*State Library of Victoria*]

all Ripper suspects, nothing has been proved. His trial lawyer, (Alfred Deakin, a future Prime Minister of Australia) attempted to mount a defence of insanity for Deeming but he was found guilty of the murder of Emily and hanged at Old Melbourne Gaol in May 1892.

BANKS GO BANG

In May 1893 the Victorian government enforced a five-day public holiday in an attempt to stop a run on local banks, many of which were about to collapse in spectacular fashion. The crash was a direct result of unregulated and over-enthusiastic financial institutions lending money on the back of the gold that had previously flowed into the city. Bankers loaned money to entrepreneurs and, especially, property speculators who were then unable to repay when land values declined, and the system collapsed. In the space of a few months 11 major Australian banks or institutions closed.

In just 17 days in May three banks closed, including the English, Scottish and Australian Chartered Bank, which, after restructuring, became the slightly shorter English, Scottish and Australian Bank before eventually merging with the Australia and New Zealand Bank to form what is today more commonly known as the ANZ Bank.

BEER STAMPEDE

When a nightwatchman at the Castlemaine Brewery premises in South Melbourne drowned in a large vat of beer in 1895, health authorities ordered that the vat be immediately emptied to prevent disease spreading. The beer flowed into the nearby

Hanna Street stormwater drain — known locally for the large number of dead cats and dogs it contained — and enterprising locals rushed to the location with containers to capture the frothy beverage. One observer described the ensuing scene as "a Bacchanalian orgy" that lasted for hours.

SEWER COLLAPSE

Six men died on Good Friday in 1895 when part of a sewer tunnel being dug under the Yarra River collapsed. As part of improvements to the Melbourne sewer network, a new tunnel was being dug to take sewage from the city to the Spotswood Pumping Station and onwards to the Werribee Sewage Farm for treatment. A shield on the tunnelling machinery failed and water flowed into the tunnel, drowning an engineer and five workers. Three other workers could see what was happening through a thick glass plate but were powerless to act. The bodies were recovered and a memorial to them now stands in Westgate Memorial Park, commemorating both this disaster and the collapse of the Westgate Bridge in 1970 when 35 workers were killed. The Spotswood Pumping Station is now part of the Scienceworks museum.

TWAIN'S VISIT

When the American writer Mark Twain arrived in Melbourne in September 1895 on a world lecture tour, his first engagement was to give a press conference to local reporters. He did this from his bedroom in the posh Menzies Hotel while laying in bed in a "cloud of tobacco smoke" in-between reading the Australian classic *For the Term of His Natural Life*. Twain's wife sat by the bed reading a romantic novel while he waxed lyrically to the reporters, prompting one of them to record that "the wife of a professional humorist has no appetite for her husbands 'chestnuts'." A little later, Twain, whose real name was Samuel Langhorne Clemens, delayed giving a lecture because of a large carbuncle that forced him to stay in bed for several days and "study wallpaper patterns."

MOTION PICTURES

The first films projected onto a screen for a paying audience anywhere in Australia were shown in August 1896 at Harry Rickards' Melbourne Opera House, later known as the Tivoli Theatre. The film, by magician Carl Hertz, was screened as part of a programme of variety acts. Australian tours with similar projection machines followed, playing at theatres until dedicated cinemas were built.

ROLLING OUT THE BARRELS

In November 1897, the 'Great Fire of Melbourne' threatened to reach the Prince's Bridge Hotel, by then owned by Henry Young and Thomas Jackson. To save the beer, a young worker at the hotel, John Connell, called for volunteers and somehow negotiated with the appropriate ecclesiastical authorities for the hotel's barrels to be rolled across Swanston Street and stored safely in the Cathedral. They were brought back the following morning, before services began.

AGE OF MERCURY

From 1899 to 1969 a four-metre-high statue of the Roman god Mercury stood on top of the *The Age* newspaper building, then in Collins Street. The statue was secured by a rod embedded three metres into a stone block and *The Age* claimed the sight was so impressive people would stop in the street and stare up at it. The statue, said to symbolise literature, science and art, was moved to the new *The Age* building in Spencer Street in 1969 for a while and then put into storage. It was loaned then finally donated to the Melbourne Museum in 1997.

St John's horse-drawn ambulance in 1901. [*State Library of Victoria*]

AMBULANCES

The first ambulance station in Melbourne was established in 1899 behind the Windsor Hotel in Spring Street. It was run by the not-for-profit St John's Ambulance Association. In 1910 they introduced motorised vehicles before later handing the service over to the new Victorian Civil Ambulance Service.

FLINDERS STREET MYTH

There is an enduring urban myth that the architectural plans for Flinders Street Station were somehow mixed up in an architect's office in London: Melbourne ended up with the building intended for Bombay (now Mumbai) and the Indian city got the one meant for Melbourne. This is easily disproved, given that the Bombay station was completed in 1888 and the final competition for a design for Flinders Street was not announced until 1899. Researchers also believe the main entrance to Flinders Street was supposed to face the end of Elizabeth Street but this was not reflected in the final plans.

Clocks above the entrance were also a notable feature of the previous station in Flinders Street. Built in 1854 and owned by the Hobson's Bay Railway Co, it was generally referred to as the City Terminus.

DOMINANT DIASPORA

Scottish immigrants and their descendants dominated much of Melbourne life during the first decades of the colony despite being only the third largest group after English and Irish arrivals. Scots were prominent in business, banking, politics, manufacturing, shipping, construction, farming, and the media. They owned or edited all of the city's major newspapers, funded schools and colleges, and — at least until 1899 — were over-represented in parliament, with an estimated 35 percent of the state's premiers having Scottish heritage.

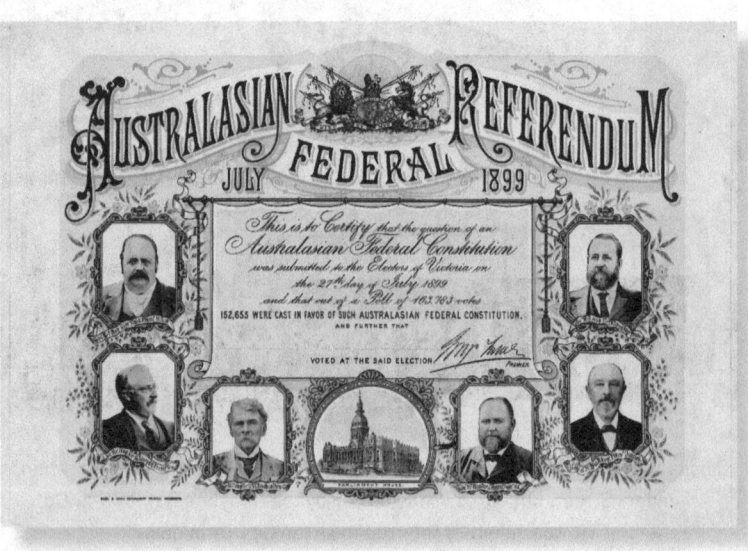

Every voter in the 1899 Federation referendum was entitled to receive a certificate like this, signed by their state Premier. This one depicts the Victoria Parliament House with the intended, but still not built, dome.
[*State Library of Victoria*]

4

1900-1939

War is declared. Motor transport arrives. Rogues and ruffians abound.

TEA AND BILLIARDS

Typical of the many lives of Melbourne buildings, 26 Flinders Street started out in 1900 as offices and storerooms for the family firm of Griffith Brothers, tea and coffee merchants. It became a newspaper office, and then for many years a billiard and snooker centre leased by the famous Lindrum family. The Lindrums had four generations of billiard champions between them, including Walter with 57 world records. After serving time as newspaper offices again, the building was redeveloped and reopened in 1999 as a boutique hotel under the Lindrum name. It is scheduled for redevelopment yet again, with only the building facade being retained and a 'mixed-use' tower block constructed behind it.

Walter Lindrum's grave in Melbourne General Cemetery in the form of a billiards table with coins lined up to reserve a game with him.

Griffiths Brothers tea house in the early 1900s, Harvie and Sutcliffe photographers. [*State Library of Victoria*]

WAR DEATH

William Lambie, a war correspondent for *The Age* newspaper in Melbourne was the first person to die in the South Africa (or Boer) War in 1900. Troops had been sent from six Australian colonies and Lambie was embedded with a contingent of Victorian and Tasmanian soldiers when he was fatally shot in the head during a surprise attack by the Boers. He had previously been a Presbyterian minister in Scotland.

THE BIG 'BAD BEER' SCARE

In January 1901, on hearing that more than 100 people had died in England after drinking 'adulterated' beer, the good citizens of Melbourne panicked that the same thing might happen to them. They fixated on brewers who added sugar to their products because it was produced from cane treated with sulphur, which might contain arsenic, and which could therefore seep into the beer itself. One writer in Melbourne *Punch* magazine was adamant sugar was the ingredient that made the beer alcoholic and unhealthy and made men drunk, whereas "pure beer made from hops and malt would have no effect whatever." Despite fierce opposite from the brewing trade, a royal commission was quickly established and drew up guidelines for beer production, but it didn't stop a 'Pure Beer' conference being held in a city hotel later that year.

WATER LOO

The first underground public toilet in Melbourne was constructed in 1902 at the junction of Bourke and Russell Streets. Although an above-ground urinal had been erected in Bourke Street in 1852 this was the first time facilities had been incorporated for women — in other words, women in the city had to hold it in for 50 years. Enthusiasm for public toilets had grown with increasing awareness of public health issues and a desire

Remains of the fence around the steps to the underground toilet at the corner of Bourke and Russell Streets.

to copy European trends. However, the Melbourne toilets only became possible because of newly available water supplies and new drainage systems throughout the city. The 1902 toilet has since been closed and covered over, with an *avant-garde* modern art installation on top, although a small portion of the original iron fencing remains.

COLERAINE TO COLLINS STREET

The international Helena Rubinstein cosmetics empire began in Melbourne in 1902 when Helena, a Jewish immigrant from Poland, opened a shop in Elizabeth Street. She had formulated a basic moisturiser and perfume while living in the country town of Coleraine, Victoria, supposedly using the plentiful lanolin from sheep farms in the Western District. Helena sold the cream through her uncle's shop to local women whose complexions were badly weathered by harsh sun and dry conditions. Once in Melbourne, her flagship product, *Crème Valaze*, sold at six shillings, about seven times the manufacturing cost of 10 pence. Her business, by then named *Maison de Beauté Valaze*, moved to premises in prestigious Collins Street and in 1908 Helena left for Europe and then America. She died in 1965 and her company ended up being bought first by Colgate-Palmolive and then, controversially, by the L'Oreal cosmetics group, whose founder, Eugéne Schueller had been a Nazi sympathiser.

SLY GROG BATTLE

In September 1904, a mass brawl broke out between rival factions of the Chinese community in Little Bourke Street. It involved revolvers, knives and clubs and, according to one newspaper report, left dozens of participants "bleeding … and all howling like dingoes." The fight between the Bo Long and Gee Hing groups started when one accused the other of informing the police about their sly-grog operations. The fighting was so vicious that many of the participants ended up in hospital with deep stab wounds. The fight was broken up by police officers called from the nearby Russell Street headquarters, in particular a Constable Barber who was observed wielding a fence post. The scene in the hospital casualty ward was described as a "particularly gory spectacle." In court the police prosecutor revealed the illegal grog was made from "tiger's bones, rice, and melon" and a government analyst said the liquid was 89 percent pure alcohol.

KILLER ELEPHANT

For four decades, Queenie, an elephant imported from India in 1905, gave joy-rides to children and adults at Melbourne Zoo until she crushed her keeper to death, probably unintentionally. Although a coronial inquest determined that she was, in fact, dangerous, she was kept on display until 1945 when zoo managers decided they could no longer afford the high cost of feed and she was euthanised.

MARCH OF THE BLUE JACKETS

Hundreds of thousands of onlookers lined the streets of central Melbourne in August 1908 to watch sailors from the American Great White Fleet march through the city. The Fleet, comprising 16 battleships and four destroyers, all painted white instead of their usual grey, was on a journey around the world with the dual objective of making courtesy calls to friendly countries while at the same time demonstrating US military power to potential adversaries. President Theodore Roosevelt was particularly concerned about the possibility of a war with Japan at the time. The Americans — nicknamed the 'blue jackets'— marched from Port Melbourne to the Exhibition Buildings for an official welcome, and then did a circuit around the city, returning to their ships by special trains from Flinders Street Station. Apart from carrying the sailors, the railways recorded their largest ever number of passengers in a single day when 400,000 Melburnians travelled into the city centre for the procession.

American sailors landing from ships ahead of their march through the city in 1908. [*US Naval History and Heritage Command*]

Cartoon by S. T. Gill, 1908. [*State Library of Victoria*]

DRIVING CRAZY

Owners of the new 'horseless carriages' were typically wealthy individuals who felt affronted by working class police officers enforcing the law in regards to their driving. The 1908 Gill cartoon reproduced above shows an encounter between a policeman and a driver who appears to have run over a cat. In 1910 there were 1590 motor cars and 1145 motorcycles registered in Victoria; of 3204 drivers who had passed their driving test, only about 100 were women. According to the latest statistics, there are currently 5.8 million registered cars, motorcycles, buses and trucks with four million licenced drivers.

A NIGHT IN GAOL

Rev. Patrick Murdoch, the most senior Presbyterian minister in Melbourne, and grandfather of media baron Rupert Murdoch, once spent a night in gaol for refusing a judge's instruction. The one time national Moderator of his denomination declined to produce a document in his church's possession at the judge's direction and in March 1909 he was gaoled for contempt. Rev. Murdoch was otherwise well-connected in Melbourne society, being personal friends with prime ministers and other senior politicians, particularly when the Federal Parliament met in Melbourne for a number of years after Federation — connections that undoubtedly proved useful when his son Keith and grandson Rupert began their media careers.

AS BENT AS

Sir Thomas Bent, who died in 1909, was a corrupt Victorian politician and one-time state Premier. He was known primarily for buying tracts of land and then arranging for tram or railway lines to be approved so that the value of the land would rise. Bent bought land to the east of Brighton and named it Bentleigh, after himself, and then arranged for the railway to be extended through the area. In one mysterious transaction he bought a block of land in Exhibition Street for £1488 and sold it later the same day for £2000. Until it was relocated in the 1970s, his statue alongside the Nepean Highway in Brighton was used by local larrikins to display the scarf and hat of the winning team of the Australian Rules Football Grand Final.

OLDE HATTERS

The olde-world hat shop next to the main entrance of Flinders Street Station has been there since 1910. City Hatters was originally the Station Master's office while the station was being built and went through a number of owners before the upmarket clothing retailer Henry Bucks bought it in 1927. As you might expect, the shop's owners say their busiest period is during the Melbourne Spring Racing Festival.

A ROARING EXIT

In February 1911 a lion named Wallace escaped from a variety show at the Opera House presented by the travelling juggler and magician 'Fasola' who was believed to be either Indian or Italian. After wandering out the back door, the lion lay down for a bit of a think in the foyer of the Temperance and General Mutual Life Assurance building in Little Collins Street. The fire brigade was

The turning or 'swing' basin at Queen's Bridge in 1927. Ships could not proceed any further along the Yarra, initially because of a low waterfall (the Yarra Falls), and, later, because of the bridge. [*State Library of Victoria*]

called but, as there was no actual fire, officers declined to help with capturing the beast. Wallace was locked inside the building foyer and despite demonstrating how loudly he could roar, was eventually coaxed into a cage borrowed from Melbourne Zoo.

CONEY ISLAND TO MELBOURNE

The popular amusement park, Luna Park, in St Kilda, was built in 1912 on the site of a failed park called Dreamland. The lease to the site was bought by American showman J. D. Williams and three brothers with the surname Phillips. They hired designers and engineers from the world-famous Coney Island amusement park in New York and replicated many of its activities and rides. The park has undergone several restorations over the years and although many of the features have been replaced, the wooden Great Scenic Railway remains the second-oldest continuously operating (apart from downtime for repairs) roller-coaster in the world and only one of a handful which still require the brakes to be operated manually by a brakeman.

UP, UP AND AWAY

The first flight from Melbourne to Sydney in an aeroplane carrying mail and commercial goods occurred on 16 July 1914. A visiting French pilot, Maurice Guillaux, volunteered at the last minute when the intended pilot was injured in a crash. Guillaux flew his Bleriot monoplane — known as a 'looper' — from Flemington Racecourse in Melbourne to Moore Park in central Sydney, where he was met by a large crowd and a band playing the Marseillaise. The flight took two days, partly due to bad weather but also because of multiple stops to refuel and perform short aerial displays. During Guillaux's earlier visit to Melbourne he had landed and taken off from the grounds of Government House. The first commercial passenger flight from Melbourne to Sydney was in 1946 in an aeroplane operated by the government-owned Trans-Australian Airlines.

TANGO TEA TIMES

The exciting new Tango dance craze arrived in Melbourne with a bang in early 1914. Despite being condemned as 'immodest' and 'immoral' by local clergy, city venues were quick to capitalise by arranging Tango Teas and Tango Suppers several times a week. A typical afternoon tea at the Opera House featured light refreshments, sometimes with ices, and a parade of brightly coloured lady's dresses. The theatre manager maintained that, if properly danced, the Tango was not vulgar, claiming "It is charming, it is graceful, it is life-giving because it brings every muscle into play."

SHOTS FIRED

The very first shot fired in World War I was directed towards a German merchant ship that left Port Melbourne in the early hours of 5 August 1914. The German ship SS *Pflaz* was trying to reach open waters before war was formally declared, when a gunnery crew at Fort Nepean received confirmation by telephone that war had indeed started and signalled the — now enemy — German ship to stop. The captain ignored this and immediately received a cannon shot across his ship's bows, the Fire Commander having been instructed to 'stop her or sink her.' The *Pflaz* turned around and the crew surrendered at Portsea. The ship was seized as a prize of war and put into service for the allies. By a remarkable coincidence, the first shot fired by Australians in World War II was from the same gun emplacement at Fort Nepean towards a ship that initially failed to identify itself but turned out to be the Australian freighter SS *Woniora*.

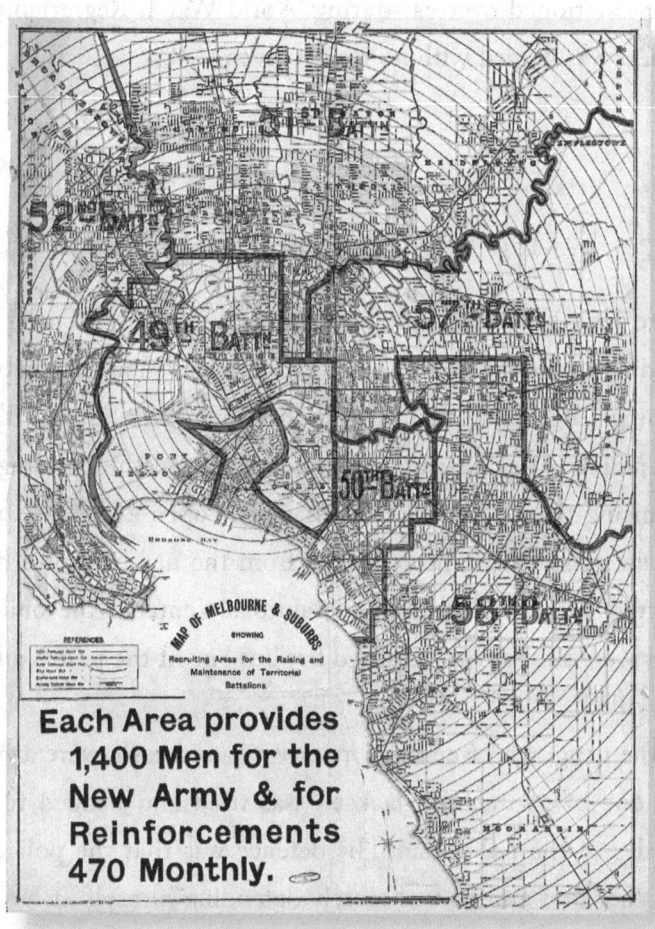

Map showing areas and target recruitment numbers for Australian troops in World War I, 1914. [*State Library of Victoria*]

DOG PARADE

In February 1916, Mr J. H. Egan, secretary of the Patriotic Dog Parade Society of Melbourne, wrote to the Lord Mayor requesting permission to parade dogs as a show of support for Australian troops stationed overseas during World War I. Regrettably, his request was denied with no reason given.

TRADES HALL SHOOTOUT

There are said to still be bullet holes in a wall of the Trades Hall building in Carlton where in 1915 there was shoot-out between criminals associated with the notorious gangster Squizzy Taylor and police. After hearing noises coming from the building and surmising them to be someone trying to open a safe, patrolling officers called for reinforcements from the nearby police headquarters in Russell Street and cautiously entered the building. They were shot at and returned fire but one of the police officers was killed.

The gang, who were after poorly-secured cash, were arrested and one of them, John Jackson was tried and hanged for the murder of the policeman. His defence was that the policeman had shot first and he was merely defending himself. It has long been rumoured that the gang were operating under orders from Squizzy Taylor and were actually after documents that proved that some trade unions were in cahoots with a rival crime gang.

NO EXCHANGE

For a brief period in 1917 the Mail Exchange building (the city postal sorting office) in Spencer Street became the official Melbourne General Post Office. The postal authorities considered the ornate GPO building in Elizabeth Street to be unfit for its purpose, not least because it was prone to serious flooding during heavy rainfall. However, after a public outcry and vitriolic letters to newspaper editors about inconvenience, official GPO status was returned to the Elizabeth Street building.

DOYLED OUT

Sir Arthur Conan Doyle, author of the Sherlock Holmes stories, arrived in Melbourne in October 1920 as part of a national tour to promote Spiritualism. Lectures were held at the Town Hall and Playhouse theatre, and included one on 'Death and the Hereafter' where some 'psychic photographs' were shown on a screen. His visit did not go down well with the local press, with a newspaper reporting one lecture was only half full. While in Melbourne he went to an Australian Rules game and a cricket match. He did not attend a horse race but noted how it seemed that "The whole population is unsettled and bent upon winning easy money." He left Australia abruptly, cancelling the Tasmanian leg of his tour because "The Stewards Union have put a spoke in my wheel."

The 3DB radio transmission masts today.

HERITAGE MASTS

The two transmission masts on the roof of the old *Herald Sun* building in Flinders Street have been there since 1921 when the newspaper company also owned radio station 3DB. They bought the station from the Druleigh Business and Technical College — hence the 'DB' in their call sign — and, in addition to the masts, sound studios and an auditorium were constructed inside the building. 3DB regularly broadcast live drama, quiz shows and variety shows and their Smileaway Club had more than 50,000 members. The station also played a major role in promoting the Royal Children's Hospital Good Friday Appeal in its early years. The station was sold in 1987 but the masts were kept and are now heritage-listed. After several changes in ownership 3DB is currently known as KIIS FM.

WRONG MAN HANGED

A man hanged for the murder of a 12-year-old girl, whose body was found in a Melbourne alley in late December 1921, was later proven to be innocent and posthumously pardoned. The murder of Alma Tirtschke resulted in a frenzy of media speculation and sensationalism, with the *Herald* newspaper offering £1000 for information leading to an arrest. Under pressure to catch the 'Gun Alley Murderer,' police arrested Colin Campbell Ross, the owner of a nearby wine bar. He was tried and found guilty of the murder of Alma on the strength of vague witness statements and a few strands of hair from blankets which supposedly matched the girl's red hair. When re-examined in 1998 using modern technology, it was found that the hairs were not, in fact, a match. A book published in 2005 claimed the killer was George Murphy, a man known to Alma's family. Ross was granted an official pardon by the state governor in 2008.

Front page of the Melbourne *Herald* on 6 January 1922

POLICE STRIKE

In October 1923, Melbourne police officers, already aggrieved about adverse pay and conditions, became angry about a new system of supervision involving plain clothes 'spooks' who would spy on them during their patrols — sometimes from behind trees and around corners. So, they went on strike. Local criminal elements took advantage of the situation and widespread looting and mass 'hooliganism' ensued. A temporary force of Special Constables, comprising many army veterans and reservists, was quickly mobilised by word of mouth and newspaper advertisements. The six-day strike ended when the authorities effectively caved in to the strikers demands but not before 636 men (out of a force of 1808) had been either dismissed or discharged. To this day it is the only time in Australia that police officers have completely withdrawn their labour.

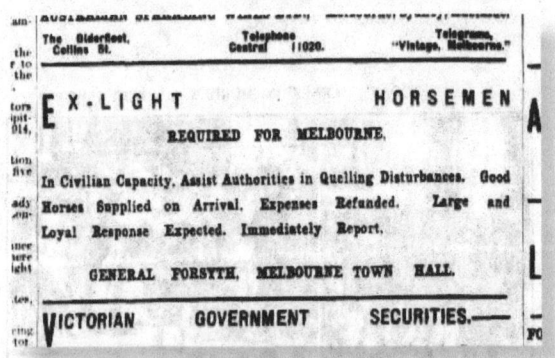

A newspaper advertisement appealing for volunteers to help quell disturbances during the police strike.

Vegemite had a different name for a few years. [*Bega Cheese Co.*]

CHEMICAL SPREAD

Iconic Australian foodstuff, Vegemite, was created by a chemist. In 1924 food manufacturer Fred Walker decided Australia needed a yeast-based spread to compete with British Marmite and asked Melbourne-based Cyril Callister to invent one. Vegemite was not an immediate success and between 1928 and 1935 it was renamed 'Parwill' in an attempt to boost sales with an advertising campaign based on a quirky pun: '*If Ma (mother) might, then Pa (father) will.*' It reverted to Vegemite and sales eventually took off when Walker obtained a licence from the American Kraft company to produce manufactured cheese in Australia and marketed them together.

A successful campaign from 1954 onwards involved children singing the "We're Happy Little Vegemites" song. Despite some media coverage, here is no truth to stories about the product being banned in overseas countries. However, it *is* prohibited from prisons in Victoria because the high yeast content could be used to make alcoholic drinks.

HOLDEN ON

Despite intense competition in later years, Holden Motors assembled car bodies for their arch rivals, Ford Motors, for several years during the early 1920s. The arrangement ended when Ford's own plant was built in Geelong in 1925. Holden also supplied 60 W-Class tramcar bodies to the Melbourne tram system and built military ambulances. When the company, by

Military ambulances produced by Holden c.1940.
[*State Library of Victoria*]

then owned by General Motors, eventually started production of a car specifically for the Australian market, they considered brand names such as Austral, Boomerang, Canbra, GeM, Emu, Melba, and Woomerah, before inevitably settling on the original Holden. The model commonly know as the FX, began selling in November 1948 for an on-road cost of about £760.

GARDENS MURDERS

The peaceful and pleasant grounds of the Botanic Gardens were the scene of an inexplicable killing spree in 1924. In the late afternoon of 21 January, Norman Alfred List, believed to be a veteran of the British army during World War I, shot five people, with four of them dying from their wounds. He had purchased a repeating rifle earlier that day from a gunsmiths in Bourke Street. At 4.30 pm he entered the Gardens and, concealed in garden beds and bushes, opened fire with deadly accuracy. The first fatality was a mother enjoying a picnic with her children, and another a father out for a stroll with his wife and children. List ran off when the rifle jammed.

The murders triggered the largest manhunt the city had ever seen, with 150 police officers tasked to find him. List was found dead from with self-inflicted wounds a few days later in heavy bush close to Pakenham, east of Melbourne. Authorities were unable to determine a reason for the murders.

END OF A LITERARY ERA

In an early example of a customer loyalty scheme, Cole's Book Arcade sold medallions or 'tokens' that gave customers special admission when the general public were excluded. The store was sometimes so crowded that entry was restricted and regular customers were given priority to one of the galleries if they had a token. Owned by eccentric Edward Cole, the Arcade began as a secondhand bookstall in 1865 in the then Eastern Market. After several changes of premises, with the business becoming larger and larger with each move, Cole ended up with a multi-level store in Bourke Street, roughly where the David Jones department store is today.

At one time the Arcade had more than two million books in stock and claimed it was the 'Grandest Bookshop in the World.' It was visited by literary celebrities such as Mark Twain and Rudyard Kipling when they were in town. After Cole died, the business declined and the shop finally closed in 1928.

STATE AND FORUM

The Forum theatre in Flinders Street was originally known as the State Theatre when it was built in 1929. The interior was deliberately designed to be 'atmospheric' with a sky blue ceiling featuring lights meant to resemble twinkling stars. The exterior

The front entrance of the Cole's Book Arcade in Bourke Street in 1890, looking towards Parliament House. [*State Library of Victoria*]

features a Moorish Revival façade replete with clocktower and minarets. During the 1990s the theatre was used by a church group before reverting to theatrical use.

GOOD FRIDAY APPEALING

The Royal Children's Hospital Foundation has raised more than $444 million since 1931 through an annual appeal to help fund the work of the Hospital. It began when a group of sports journalists, concerned about the possibility of the hospital having to close, held a carnival procession and series of sporting events and raised a total of £427. The appeal became an annual event and

A familiar sign on demolition sites from 1923 onwards, as yet another bit of the city's past disappeared. [*Museums Victoria*]

moved to Good Friday in 1942 when radio station 3DB agreed to the first all-day broadcast of a money-raising 'radiothon.' The hospital itself began in 1839 in a residential house in Stephen Street (later renamed Exhibition Street) and had six patient beds. It had an all-women Board of Management.

PUPPY DOG CORNER

A corner of Swanston and Collins Streets was once known as 'Puppy Dog Corner' because of the many lovestruck couples who arranged to meet outside the jewellery shop there. Bought by the Manchester Unity Independent Order of Oddfellows in 1932 the shop was demolished and the Manchester Unity Building constructed in an Art Deco Gothic style. It contained Melbourne's first escalators, high-speed lifts and toilets for both sexes. It also had a rooftop garden with a café. In 1978, on the eighth floor, three jewellers were murdered and $30,000 stolen in a case that has never been solved.

NOISE COMPLAINT

In 1933, when traffic and street noises were much lower than they are today and sound travelled further, residents of Carlton complained to the management of Melbourne Zoo, some two kilometres away in Parkville, that they were being woken much too early each morning by the sound of hungry lions roaring for their breakfast. Bemused zoo officials explained there was little they could do.

The collection of shop fronts on the Lonsdale Street side of the Myer store in 1929 (now the Emporium centre). [*State Library of Victoria*]

STREET NAMES

The stretch of Swanston Street in Carlton between Victoria Street and the University of Melbourne was originally known as Madeline Street. The old name stuck firmly with locals who found it very difficult to change. So, when a newly born baby girl was found abandoned near the Women's Hospital in 1934 the staff named her Madeline Carlton. The name of another city street, Stephen Street, was changed to Exhibition Street in 1880 after residents complained it had become associated with criminal activity and prostitution. It was named for the International Exhibition being held that year — but only from Collins Street northwards, the southern section, down to Flinders Street, was called Collins Place until 1963.

WOMEN ONLY

From 1934 to 1957, the women-only Lyceum Club — the only such club in Melbourne — rented the top two floors of the 'Gothic Bank' building in Collins Street, once the home of the English, Scottish and Australian Bank, and then the international headquarters of ANZ Bank before it moved to Docklands. The lavishly designed rooms had previously been the private residence of the bank's general manager. The dining room featured a turret with a line of sight to the Yarra turning basin so he could check for newly-arrived ships that might owe the bank money. The Lyceum was founded in 1912, predominantly for female graduates from the University of Melbourne, and now exists for any woman with university qualifications involved in art, literature, music, education or significant public service.

BENDING THE LIGHT

When the Shrine of Remembrance in St Kilda Road was completed in 1934 it featured a ray of light falling on the word 'love' in an inscription on the Shrine floor. It was carefully planned that this would occur at 11 am on the eleventh day of the eleventh

The beam of light at the Melbourne Shrine.

month — when fighting in World War I ceased. However, when daylight saving was introduced in Victoria in 1972 the light beam became an hour out of synch and fell on the inscription at midday instead. To rectify this, artificial light was used and then in 1976 mirrors were installed in the roof to redirect the beam. Alignment of the mirrors is checked every year because of slight movements in the building.

TRUST US WITH YOUR BUB

From 1935, young mothers from the suburbs were encouraged to leave their children in the care of railway staff at Flinders Street Station while they shopped in the city. The Railways Department had established a 'modern and well appointed nursery' on the

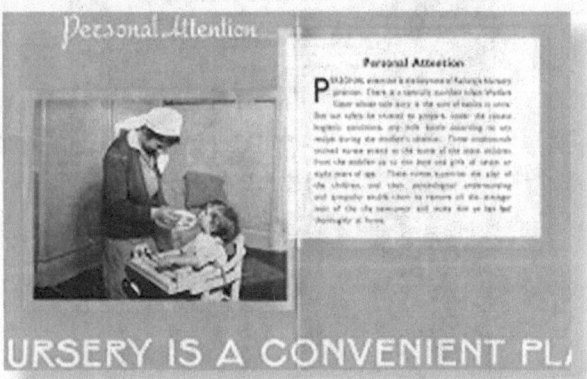

A brochure promising "personal attention" to babies left at Flinders Street Station nursery.

The University lake, c.1930s. [*University of Melbourne Archives*]

second floor of the building and advertised that it had 'fresh air, ventilation and central heating' throughout. Nursery staff were 'qualified and experienced' and charged sixpence for an hour's childcare and up to two shillings for a whole day. The nursery was closed in 1942 due to concerns about groups congregating in the city during World War II.

LAKESIDE MANNERS

Run, don't walk. There was once a large ornamental lake in the centre of the University of Melbourne grounds in Parkville. It was excavated in the early days of the University and the meandering Bouverie Creek allowed to flow into it. Children from nearby streets became used to crossing the grounds at a swift pace because some students found it amusing to push them into the lake. It was filled in during the late 1930s to make way for a new chemistry building.

WHOOSH!

In the 1930s, sales assistants at the Myer department store used capsules in pneumatic tubes to whisk cash to a central money handling office upstairs. Change and a receipt would be returned via the same tubes. Some supermarkets still use a modern version of this system to transport cash from checkouts to a secure room but none are as extensive as the estimated 40 miles of tubing installed at Myer. The pneumatic system exchange unit is still visible on Level 6 of the Bourke Street store.

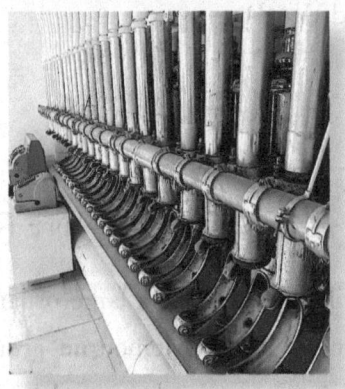

The remains of the elaborate pneumatic cash handling system at the Myer department store in Bourke Street.

ANTI-ANTI-FASCISTS

The crew of an Italian navy warship visiting Melbourne in February 1938 were enraged when they found Italian emigrants in the city distributing anti-fascist literature. They attacked and severely injured a taxi-driver who went on board the ship during its open day when they thought they recognised him as one of those handing out leaflets at an Italian club in Carlton. As a result, several thousand (reports put the number at between 7000 and 10,000) local Italians descended on Princes Pier where the *Raimondo Montecuccoli* was docked but were blocked by mounted and foot police. They burnt an effigy of the fascist Italian leader Mussolini and made speeches denouncing fascism. Authorities declined to take any action against the crew because the ship was considered official Italian territory.

BEST THING SINCE

Melbourne can arguably claim to have produced the first sliced bread anywhere in the world. A bakery in the town of Chillicothe, Missouri, in the USA, started to produce slices with a machine in 1928, and in Australia the Sunshine bakery in Newtown, Sydney followed, with sliced and packaged bread being sold from 1939 onwards. However, the Victorian Railways Refreshment Services Branch bakery had been selling pre-packed slices of raisin bread at breakfast time since 1923. The branch was responsible for all the tea rooms at railway stations and ran the refreshment buffets and carts on long-distance trains. Production of all pre-packed bread in Australia stopped when restrictions were put on the use of packaging materials during World War II but recommenced in 1958 with the national *Tip Top* brand and the growth of self-serve supermarkets.

5

1940–1999

Another war. Immigration surges. The city modernises and expands.

ARMS CROSSED

For nearly 100 years the City of Melbourne used a heraldic Coat of Arms without proper permission — yet no one seemed to notice. The Arms were based on the previous town Common Seal and in addition to a crown and the red cross of St George, depicted a sheep's fleece, a bull, a whale and a three-masted ship, all important aspects of the local economy at that time. However, for some mysterious reason, although passed by the city council in 1843, formal approval was not sought until late 1939. In the meantime it could have been used by anyone or, as one city councilor put it, as a label on a jam jar.

The College of Heralds in London, the ancient body responsible for such things, denied but then grumpily granted a royal licence in January 1940, pointing out that the Coat of Arms did not meet its high standards. Its two glaring errors being that it should not be using an imperial crown, and the two water-based emblems should be positioned on the same level, not one above the other. Nevertheless, the King of Arms eventually relented and issued a licence once the council had paid the appropriate fee (£130).

In 1970 the Arms were again adjusted, with the water features finally moved to the same level and two gold 'supporter' lions and other embellishments added. The new Coat of Arms (or, more properly, the Armorial Bearings) received official approval from London and Letters Patent were handed to the Lord Mayor by Queen Elizabeth II during her visit in April 1970.

The old, pre-1970, City of Melbourne Coat of Arms on Princes Bridge.

THE BROWNOUT STRANGLER

The brutal night-time murders of three women in May 1942 saw dramatic newspaper reports focus on the hunt for the 'Brownout Strangler.' During World War II Melbourne residents and businesses were required to reduce the amount of light coming from their premises because of concerns about possible night-time aerial attacks by Japanese aeroplanes. The regulations were not as extensive as Britain's wartime 'blackouts' and were referred to locally as 'brownouts.' However, the darkened city streets were believed to be a contributory factor in the serial killings. A visiting US serviceman, Private Eddie Leonski, was arrested and tried under US military regulations and hanged at Pentridge Prison in November the same year.

CAMP MURPHY

In 1942, and again in 1943, personnel from the US Army Fifth Air Force and elements of the US Marine Corps were stationed at the Melbourne Cricket Ground. The temporary barracks were officially called 'Cricket Grounds' and unofficially 'Camp Murphy' in honour of a US Air Force officer killed in Java. Tents were erected around the edge of the oval — because even in wartime nothing was allowed to disturb the hallowed turf.

"I wish you'd told me before, you were marrying someone else, Mabel."

Being away from your loved one for lengthy periods could have serious consequences for your relationship, 1942. [*State Library of Victoria*]

TUNNEL MYTHS

There are dozens of rumours and urban myths about tunnels and secret underground rooms in Melbourne but, regrettably, hardly any of them are true. For example, there is supposedly a network of military bunkers under Royal Park, built when American troops were camped there during World War II. When a couple of sink holes appeared in the park, it sent tunnel believers into a frenzy of excitement, but no network was found. There are also believed to be tunnels criss-crossing the city in various locations, from bank headquarters to branches, and from the Treasury building to banks downtown.

There could be lost rooms under Manchester House in Flinders Lane still containing gold from the gold rush era. The hidden bowling alley under Degraves Street might be entered via an old telephone booth. Unsurprisingly, Crown Casino officials confirm there are no hidden passages leading from certain toilet cubicles to a secret morgue to transport suicide cases.

Some believe that during World War II a boat was permanently moored on the Yarra close to Flinders Street Station so, in the event of an attack, military commanders and members of the war cabinet could be whisked to a secret bunker alongside the Merri Creek in Westgarth. While a bunker did exist (and has since been filled in) no-one seems to know what it was for, and it would be impossible anyway because a boat could not navigate upstream over Dights Falls in Abbotsford.

SERENDIPITY DIM SIMS

The now iconic Australian 'dim sim' was created accidentally. By the 1940s, Cantonese *dim sum* dumplings had become widely available in Melbourne, especially the pot-shaped, pork and prawn *siu mai*, also known as the more easily pronounceable *dim sim*. Then, around 1945, a dim sim maker, on his way to deliver a box of his dumplings, called in to see friend who owned a fish and chip shop. The friend persuaded him to join him on a fishing trip for the rest of the day and on their return, rather than waste the dim sims, the pair decided to deep fry them. Other friends started asking where they could get them and soon dim sims were available at almost every fish and chip shop, with the famous South Melbourne Market version becoming much widely sought-after.

WOMEN'S WORK

During World War II (1939-1945) most of the explosives and ammunition supplied to troops from munitions factories in Melbourne were produced by women. A large gunpowder storage facility known as 'Jack's Magazine' had existed in Footscray next to the Maribyrnong River since 1878 on land that had once been a stud farm and racecourse, and an armaments industry grew up around it. It has also been claimed that all of the bullets used by Australian troops at Gallipoli and on the Somme battlefield in

Working in a munitions factory, 1940. [*National Archives of Australia*]

World War I were made in the area. With many male workers drafted into military service, the government instituted a forced recruitment scheme for remaining citizens over the age of 18 years and many women opted to work in the munitions factories making ammunition, bombs, and other explosives. The main building of Jack's Magazine has been preserved and is now on the heritage register.

MURDER MAGNET

In August 1948 Melbourne police successfully deployed state-of-the-art technology during a search for a murder weapon after a man was found dead in the Maribyrnong River. They borrowed a heavy-duty magnet from police in New South Wales and dragged it along the river bed. They found an iron bar that led to the conviction of Eric Jacobi for the murder of 19-year-old Norman Hurley, whose body was found floating in the river at Flemington. Although Jacobi was found guilty and sentenced to hang, the sentence was later commuted with no reason given at the time.

Snow falling in August, 1951 at the intersection of Collins and Swanston Streets. [*Fairfax Archives*]

COLOUR FIRST

On Monday 28 July 1952, Melbourne newspaper *The Argus* became the first paper anywhere in the world to print a full colour 'action' photograph on its front page. The photo was of a horse race at the Moonee Valley track. Another colour photo on the back page featured an Australian Rules football match between Fitzroy and Collingwood.

WHEELY GOOD IDEA

The first Meals on Wheels service in Australia began in South Melbourne in 1953 when a Miss E. Watts used a tricycle to transport a large 'hot box' containing eight meals for elderly or infirm residents. There was a small charge of one shilling and three pence for the food and another three pence for delivery. The tricycle and box used by Miss Watts were donated by the local Home Help Auxiliary and the following year the Red Cross organisation stepped in, supplying a car and additional volunteers. Despite a slight decline over the years, the latest available figures for Meals on Wheels services throughout Australia show that more than 14 million meals are being delivered annually by nearly 79,000 volunteers.

FISHY FIRE

In addition to the large main hall, the Exhibition Buildings in Carlton Gardens once contained a ballroom, a large aquarium, a mus-eum, and cinemas. The aquarium burnt down one evening in January 1953. Thousands of exotic fish and reptiles perished when red-hot metal sheets fell from the roof into their tanks and enclosures. One of the prized specimens killed was a Japanese Salamander which, according to legend, can live in fire. Despite volunteers trying to coax them out, two seals spent the entire time circling their pool while embers fell on them. The alarm was raised by two young boys, aged 7 and 11 years, who saw the flames and called out to a nightwatchman. Authorities said afterwards that if the boys had not acted quickly the entire Exhibition building would have been destroyed.

ROYAL BOOMERANGS

For the visit of newly crowned Queen Elizabeth II in 1954, an archway featuring a pair of huge boomerangs with a crown above them was erected towards the top end of Bourke Street. In the photograph opposite, the Victorian Parliament House can be seen bearing an 'EIIR' crest framed by the Boomerangs. The Queen visited Melbourne several times during her reign, the final time being in 2011.

The boomerang arch, 1954. [*State Library of Victoria*]

ESPRESSO RIVALS

Who was first? The owners of the Il Capuccino [*sic*] cafe in St Kilda claimed they were the first to import an espresso machine (in 1954), while the Mirka Café in Exhibition Street maintained they were the first to use a commercial machine the same year. Mirka's also claim to have been the first café in the city with chairs and tables on the footpath outside. However, Pellegrini's in Bourke Street and the University Café in Lygon Street have long vied for the honour of being the first 'proper' continental-style 'espresso bar.' While there had been a number of 'coffee lounges' previously, they had used a filter or percolation method, not a 'proper' espresso machine.

HOME FOR A PRESS

Wealthy Melbourne industrialist, Russell Grimwade, bequeathed his large and prestigious Toorak property called 'Miegunyah' to publishing entity Melbourne University Press when he died in 1955 with the intention that it should become its offices and printery. He believed it would facilitate the production of high quality books along the lines of the Clarendon Press at Oxford University. However, the premises were unsuitable for this purpose and the property was sold, with the proceeds placed in a fund to subsidise production of high quality scholarly books. The first title published under the new Miegunyah Press imprint in 1967 was a biography of Sir Russell himself. Since then there have been more than 240 titles with many of them winning literary awards. 'Miegunyah' is derived from an Aboriginal word supposedly meaning shelter.

TELEVISION BEGINS

Melbourne television stations began test transmissions within a few months of each other in 1956, just in time to cover the Melbourne Olympic Games. The HSV-7 (Channel 7) call sign was based on the names of its two newspaper owners: The *Herald* and the *Sun*. Its rival GTV-9 (General Television Victoria — Channel 9) was owned by a consortium that included *The Age*

The Argus folds on same day Channel 9 is launched in 1957.

and *The Argus* newspapers, and ABV became the non-commercial public broadcaster ABC (originally the Australian Broadcasting Commission, now Corporation). Ironically, *The Argus* closed down on the same day GTV-9 was formally launched in January 1957. Their brand new studios in Richmond had previously been a Heinz tinned food factory and before that, a piano-making factory. Their offices and studios have since moved to the Docklands district, close to Southern Cross Station.

OLYMPIC GAMES

The 1956 Olympic Games in Melbourne were nearly cancelled three times. After winning the right to stage the games by just one vote in 1949, Olympic officials regularly visited the city and were increasingly dismayed by the slow pace of building the necessary facilities and threatened to cancel the entire event. The Games themselves were marred by Cold War tensions when several European countries refused to attend because of the Soviet Union's recent suppression of the Hungarian uprising. During the Games, a water polo game between Russia and Hungary became violent and bloody. China also refused to attend because Taiwan had been invited. Australia's strict quarantine laws meant that for the first time an Olympic sport was held outside the host country when equestrian events were moved to Stockholm, Sweden. The famous annual Myer Christmas window displays were introduced in 1956 to celebrate the Olympics.

An electric Olympic torch outside Flinders Street Station during the Games, 1956. [*National Archives of Australia*]

The new 'Paris' end of Collins Street.

THE PARIS END

Referring to the eastern end of Collins Street as the 'Paris End' can be dated to 1957 when, Leon Ress, owner of the opulent Oriental Hotel, successfully applied for a permit to place 19 tables and chairs on the wide footpath outside the hotel. It helped that he was also a city councillor because a previous owner's application had been dismissed out of hand. Ress's wife, born in Paris, told newspaper reporters that it was just like the Champ-Élysées back home and, even though the permit was revoked two years later, the idea stuck. It was not the first pavement café in Melbourne — that honour belongs to Mirka's, on the corner of Exhibition and Little Bourke Streets (see page 117).

Rev. Graham preaching at the MCG, 1959. [*The Billy Graham Center Archives at Wheaton College*]

BILLY'S BIG BASH

After holding 24 meetings, American preacher Billy Graham, finished his evangelistic 'Crusade' in March 1959 with a record-breaking rally at the Melbourne Cricket Ground (MCG). The event drew an estimated crowd of 143,750 people, many of whom spilled on to the grassed area. It remains the largest attendance at the MCG for any type of event.

CASH IN TRANSIT

In the 1950s, when trains carried cash and other valuables, armed train guards practised their shooting skills at a small underground pistol range under the then Spencer Street railway station.

FAKE ESPRESSO GIRL

In 1961, the tabloid *Truth* newspaper ran a series of sensational articles about how the growing number of migrant-run espresso bars in the city were being used as a cover for prostitution and other illegal activities. The story was reinforced by interviews with 'Jill,' who claimed to have been lured into a life of crime through the bars, the details of which were then broadcast on radio and television. But 'Espresso Bar Girl' was fake. It was later admitted that 'Jill' had fabricated her story in cahoots with police who had wanted to bring the bars into some kind of disrepute and were encouraged by newspapers trying to increase circulation with sensationalist reporting.

MINI OUTRAGE

While it is well known that visiting fashion super-model Jean Shrimpton outraged racegoers on Melbourne's Derby Day in 1965 by wearing a 'mini' skirt with the hem a whole 10 cms above her knees, the *Sun News-Pictorial* reported that onlookers were equally horrified by the fact she was wearing "NO hat, NO gloves and NO stockings." The Shrimp wryly observed that perhaps conservative Melbourne was not ready for her — or London fashion — just yet.

MODS AND SHARPIES

Bitter youth sub-culture rivals in the mid-sixties, Melbourne 'Mods' and 'Sharpies' echoed similar movements in Britain where they were called 'Mods' and 'Rockers.' Often descending into violent clashes whenever they met, the groups were identified by their clothing choices, with the Mods favouring a look similar to *The Beatles* in the early 1960s and, later, the Californian hippy movement. Sharps typically dressed in denim and jeans, particularly *Levi's* and *Lee* brands. Unlike their British counterparts both sets liked the music of both *The Beatles* and the *Rolling Stones*. In 2006, and ignoring past violent undertones, *Levi's* introduced a Black Sharps retro fashion range that deliberately referenced sixties culture.

THE FAB FIVE

The first and only time *The Beatles* appeared in public with *five* members was in 1964 at the Southern Cross Hotel in Collins Street during their Australian tour. Drummer Ringo Starr had become ill with tonsillitis just before the tour began and was temporarily replaced by Jimmy Nichol for several concerts in Melbourne before Ringo resurfaced. All five then attended a press conference on 14 June. An estimated 30,000 adoring teenagers gathered outside the hotel, screaming hysterically while hoping to catch sight of their idols. A Channel 9 television reporter, visibly shaken by the commotion, angrily told viewers "if your child is out there, you should be ashamed."

GREEN PAINT PROTEST

When American President Lyndon Johnson made a side-trip to South Yarra during his 1966 visit, a group of anti-Vietnam War protesters pelted his car with green paint. A white business shirt worn by a US Secret Service agent accompanying the President was splattered with the paint and is among the many oddities in the care of the Melbourne Museum. The student protesters were arrested and charged, and their lawyer later wrote to the President to apologise for their actions.

DISPOSSESSED APOSTROPHES

In 1966, a state government agency, the Geographic Names Board (now called Geographic Names Victoria), decided that no place name in the state should have a possessive apostrophe. Thus, Prince's Bridge became Princes Bridge, Queen's Bridge became Queens Bridge, Fisherman's Bend became, absurdly, Fishermans Bend, and so on. However, most buildings, particularly churches named after saints, have kept their apostrophe.

END OF THE SWILL

Finally abolished in 1966, the 'six o'clock swill' flowed from legislation passed in 1916 prohibiting pubs and hotels from selling alcohol after 6 pm. Workers would crowd into city pubs after work and attempt to drink as much as they could before closing time. Drunken patrons would then stagger out and make their way home on foot or by public transport. The mêlée inside hostelries as people jostled and elbowed their way to the bar to get served was described by a visitor to the city as being like a 'pig's swill.' The legislation had been introduced during World War I as a way of improving public moral and had also been encouraged by the temperance movement which had been lobbying for restrictions since the 1870s.

FIND-A-STREET

The first edition of the iconic *Melways* street directory was published in 1966. It took five years to hand-draw all the roads and other features and sold for £2.50, twice the price of its nearest competitor. It was launched by television star Graham Kennedy on Channel 9's *In Melbourne Tonight* show and was an immediate success. The founders soon realised that they would have to produce a new edition every year to keep pace with the rapid growth of Melbourne suburbs.

IT'S A SIGN

The removal in 1968 of 'Little Audrey,' a neon sign advertising a brand of vinegar, led to a public outcry by locals and a Friends of Audrey group began a campaign for its return. The sign, which depicts a young girl with a skipping rope which appears to be moving, was first placed above a factory in Victoria Street, Abbotsford in 1936 but unceremoniously removed when the building was demolished. In 1970 the owner of a nearby factory arranged for a smaller reproduction to be made and this was placed on the roof. The sign is referenced in many works of popular culture, and the second version has been placed on the Victorian Heritage Register. It is currently powered by solar panels. An image of a skipping Little Audrey also appears on the labels of Cornwell's brand vinegar bottles.

Little Audrey in her current location.

PERSIAN RUG OF LIGHT

The largest stained-glass ceiling in the world is housed in the Great Hall of the National Gallery of Victoria in St Kilda Road, which opened to the public in August 1968. The ceiling comprises 16,000 individual pieces of diamond-cut glass, contained within 224 triangular frames, each weighing 300 kilograms. Designed by Australian artist Leonard French, it took approximately five years to complete. Referred to affectionately as a 'Persian Rug of Light,' visitors frequently resort to laying on the floor to fully appreciated it.

TAME TIGERS TURFED

In May 1969, the Melbourne city health department ordered the removal of two tame tigers residing in the backyard of the upmarket Belzac restaurant in East Melbourne. They had been placed there by a former circus trainer who felt sorry for them because they had to dive into water that was 'too cold' as part of an act at Ashton's Circus. The tigers were taken to a new home on five acres of land in Warburton. The owner of the restaurant said that he got on 'very well indeed' with the tigers while they were there.

HORSE PARKING

Horse-hitching posts were common throughout the city during the 1800s but, as motor vehicle use gained momentum in the early 1900s, they gradually disappeared. Melbourne City Council thoughtfully kept one post that had stood on the kerb outside a house in Spring Street and in 1971 relocated it to Treasury Gardens. It now stands on the north-east corner of Spring Street and Wellington Parade. Horse drinking troughs were another common feature in the city, many of them paid for by animal welfare activists. One remaining example of a trough can be seen partly hidden by a flower bed outside the McDonald's restaurant in Clifton Hill.

The old horse-hitching post in Treasury Gardens.
[*City of Melbourne Heritage Collection*]

TRAFALGAR LINK

A ship's anchor swivel, which has sat without fanfare in a park in Williamstown since 1974, once belonged to a ship that fought at the famous Battle of Trafalgar. The swivel was last attached to Her Majesty's Victorian Ship *Nelson*, a gunboat given to the colony by British authorities to help form a naval fleet of its own. It had previously been used on HMS *Bellerophon*, a double-deck, 74-gun warship that fought alongside Admiral Horatio Nelson's HMS *Victory* at the battle in 1805. The *Bellerophon* — nicknamed the *Billy Ruffian* because sailors found it difficult to pronounce — was also the ship on which Emperor Napoléon Bonaparte surrendered in July 1815 (after several days of negotiations) and which then took him to England before he was exiled on the small island of St Helena in the South Atlantic ocean.

THE GREAT BOOKIE ROBBERY

In April 1976, six men with machine-guns robbed the offices of the Victoria Club in Queen Street where bookmakers were settling up after horse races run over the Easter weekend. It is estimated that anywhere between $1.5 and $15 million was stolen and none of it has ever been recovered. Intriguingly, no-one has ever been charged with the crime even though the names of several suspects were revealed by a lawyer connected to the case. Most of the alleged gang members had been murdered by the end of 1987 and the remaining suspect was killed in a police shoot-out during another heist in 1992.

PHOSPHATE TOWER

In 1977, the government of the tiny Pacific republic of Nauru invested the considerable profits from phosphate mining on the island in a new office tower at 80 Collins Street. The phosphate is formed from centuries of droppings from migrating birds and led to the building being nicknamed 'Birdshit House.'

ELVIS GROTTO

The Melbourne General Cemetery in Carlton contains a large memorial to American singer and entertainer Elvis Presley who died in Memphis, Tennessee, in 1977. Commissioned by the President of the Australian Elvis Presley Fan Club a few months after his death, the monument and grotto draws hundreds of visitors every year, many coming on the anniversary of his death on 16 August.

The *Cavalcade of Transport* mural hiding at the rear of a shop.

FOLLOW THE CAVALCADE

Commissioned by the Victorian government for $250,000 and unveiled in 1978, *Cavalcade of Transport* is a large and colourful mural depicting the first century of public transport in Victoria. At 38 metres wide, it had pride of place above the ticketing offices at the old Spencer Street Station. When the station was redeveloped and renamed Southern Cross, the mural was relocated to a wall at the rear of the upstairs shopping centre where it could be viewed, along with a panel explaining all the various sections. However, the mural has now effectively disappeared behind shops built in front of the wall. To see it, you must enter one of the stores (during opening hours) and find your way past the shelves and clothes racks to the back wall.

INSPIRING

To save money, the soaring spire of the Arts Centre in St Kilda Road, erected in 1984, was built significantly shorter than originally designed. However, when it was refurbished in 1996, improvements in engineering technology and materials meant it could be increased to 162 metres with a 10 metre mast on top — well above the originally 126 metres planned in the eighties. The lower portion of the gold, silver and white design is intended to resemble the flowing folds of a ballerina's dress. The total weight of steel in the spire and mast is nearly 98 tonnes.

DUST COVER

In February 1983, a massive and dramatic dust storm, on a scale similar to those that periodically engulf middle-eastern cities, hit Melbourne, covering it in red dust and dirt. Soil had been swept up by high winds from the Mallee district in western Victoria and carried towards Melbourne. Approximately 50,000 tonnes of top soil was stripped away and between 3.00 pm and about 4.00 pm a considerable amount of it landed on Melbourne. People reported not being able to see more than 100 metres in front of them; trains stopped and Tullamarine and Essendon Airports temporarily closed. Hundreds suffered breathing difficulties, but no deaths were recorded.

GUNS AND BALACLAVAS

In November 1983, an anti-terrorism training exercise involving junior agents of the Australian Secret Intelligence Service (ASIS) went spectacularly awry and ended the career of its Director-General. The organisation neglected to inform management or guests at the Sheraton Hotel in Spring Street of the exercise which involved operatives wearing balaclava masks, breaking down a door with a sledgehammer and threatening staff with pistols and sub-machine guns fitted with silencers. The hotel manager, believing a robbery was taking place, called police who arrested several of the agents as they tried to flee.

A federal government investigation blamed the Director-General, John Ryan, for not warning anyone in advance and he promptly resigned. The Victorian Director of Public Prosecutions considered laying charges against those involved but decided there was insufficient evidence to convict any individual.

LONG AND DEEP

The three underground stations of the City Loop railway — Flagstaff, Museum (later renamed Melbourne Central), and Parliament — were opened in stages between 1981 and 1985. They have a total of 48 escalators serving platforms in four tunnels. The deepest station is Parliament which is 40 metres below ground and which currently has the longest (and possibly scariest) escalator in the Southern Hemisphere at 30 metres.

GREENING SWANSTON STREET

In February 1985, as part of Victoria's centenary celebrations, four blocks of Swanston Street, the city's main thoroughfare, were carpeted with real grass. An estimated 500,000 people visited the city over the course of a weekend to walk on the grass and enjoy performances on five stages along the street. The outstanding success of the event led (after much debate) to vehicle-congested Swanston Street becoming the semi-pedestrian-only precinct it is today and the initiative is considered a major factor in the revitalisation of the city centre.

Crowds walking on the grass 'carpet' in Swanston Street in 1985. [*Victorian Ministry of Planning*]

SHELL HOUSES

Completed in 1989, Shell House, at 1 Spring Street, is one of the few buildings in Australia designed by prestigious international architect Harry Seidler. When viewed from above, the building forms part of the shape of the sea-shell logo of the Royal Dutch Shell oil company who used it as their Australian headquarters until it was sold and turned into apartments. Shell had previously occupied other office buildings in the city centre: Shell Corner, designed in 1958, at the junction of Bourke and William Streets, and before that, Old Shell Building in William Street, designed in 1932.

JAPANESE OUTLET

When the Melbourne Central shopping centre opened in 1991, it was dominated by a branch of the major Japanese department store chain Daimaru, which took up six upper floors of the complex. However, a downturn in the Japanese economy meant they could no longer afford to compete with the rival city-centre Myer and David Jones department stores, and they exited the centre in 2002, paying $30 million to break their lease. Although the centre was remodelled and other outlets took Daimaru's place, there is still evidence of its relatively brief existence, such as the remains of escalator landing platforms on upper levels but no actual escalators leading to them.

NEW PUNT

Punts and ferries across the Yarra River have been gradually replaced by bridges of one kind or another, but in 1993 a brand new one started up. The Westgate Punt takes foot passengers and cyclists from Westgate Landing at the end of Lorimer Street, Port Melbourne, across to the Spotswood Jetty near Scienceworks museum. The fare is currently $3 on weekdays and $5 at weekends.

BIKE PATHS

There are approximately 1900 kms of bike paths or trails in the Melbourne area, with about 135 kms in the city alone. The first dedicated cycle lane installed in Melbourne was on St Kilda Road in 1993. However, at five kilometres long it was constantly criticised because cyclists had to ride in the door-opening zone of parked cars. The lanes have since been reconstructed and separated from traffic to provide better protection for the estimated 3500 bike riders who use them every day. Dedicated lanes and paths now total 1900 kms around Melbourne and are popular because of the city's relatively flat terrain and temperate climate. Many of them run alongside picturesque creeks and rivers.

MAGIC SECRETS

The State Library holds the collection of Mr W. G. Alma, a renowned Australian magician who died in 1993. It contains secrets of magic and conjuring tricks and, although the Library is acceding to Mr Alma's request not to put some of the secrets on open display, the collection can still be viewed on request.

COFFEE FIRST THING

The first McCafé in the world opened at the front of a (now demolished) McDonald's restaurant in Swanston Street in 1993. It was created by Ann Brown, the franchisee, with encouragement from senior managers at McDonald's headquarters. The McCafé in-store coffee shop concept has since been rolled out around the world with more than 4000 outlets in 60 countries. It has been estimated that one in four coffees in Australia are bought from a McDonald's McCafé every day.

ON TRACKS

The quirkiest installation in the City of Melbourne collection of works of art must surely be the Railway Viewing Platform in North Melbourne. Installed in 1994, it looks west and south

The Railway Viewing Platform installation, North Melbourne.

over a complex system of rail tracks approaching Southern Cross Station. The council says it pays homage to trainspotters and to "the moving, grinding, squealing 'ships on wheels'."

CONNIES GONE

In 1998, after more than 100 years on cable cars and then electric trams, human conductors were replaced by automated ticketing machines. Known affectionately as 'connies' these men and women not only sold tickets but assisted passengers with journey information, helped the elderly and passengers with disabilities, and provided security at night. Some were known for bursts of song, poetry or short dramatic performances that kept passengers entertained on their journey.

THE HARRODS OF MELBOURNE

Georges, at the 'Paris' end of Collins Street, was the poshest department store in Melbourne until it closed in 1995. In its heyday the store had departments to suit the needs of every wealthy person in the city, including one that catered specifically for slim people aged 16 to 60 years. During the opulent 1880s the store presented Punch and Judy shows, 'amusements' at Christmas, and arranged special sessions for women who wanted to learn to ride bicycles. According to one report, when the store closed after 115 years, loyal customers were heard to mutter that it wasn't the store that had been unsuccessful, but Melbourne itself, having failed to live up to its high standards.

TILLY BELLS

Among the many statues and monuments in Kings Domain gardens is a sculpture dedicated to Tilly Aston, a blind disability activist and poet who helped to establish a braille library. She is said to be the first blind person to have attended university in Australia. The sculpture, erected in 1999, is in the shape of three interconnecting bells and when approached a sensor is meant to trigger a series of bell tolls. Regrettably, the sensors no longer work and the bells are silent.

6

2000-2024

The city evolves and reaches upwards. Things go digital. Heritage in jeopardy.

A STICK UP

Visitors travelling into the city from Melbourne Airport are invariable intrigued by the single bright yellow beam jutting out at a precarious angle over the 'International Gateway' end of the CityLink freeway. Erected in 2000, it was inspired by the Victorian Gold Rush, and the 39 smaller, bright red beams next to it represent the state's wheat industry. Who knew? Not many, apparently. Locals call it 'The Cheesestick' or 'The Big Chip.'

TRIANGLES AND BUNKERS

The massive concrete 'deck' on which Federation Square sits took 12 months to build and contains 1.4 kilometres of concrete 'crash walls,' 3000 tonnes of steel beams, extensive rubber padding and more than 4000 springs to absorb vibrations from trains passing

Exterior wall cladding, Federation Square.

underneath. When it opened in 2002, the square was considered one of Australia's most unusual and ambitious building projects and regarded as a 'perfectly executed' feat of modern engineering. The design of the cladding on the building façades is based on large, triangular panels which are progressively divided into smaller triangles. These incorporate three different building materials: sandstone, zinc and glass.

The original plan for the square called for a visitor's centre with elevated glass shards to be built on the north-east corner but this idea was abandoned because it would have obscured the view of St Paul's Cathedral. One of the square's buildings, the Australian Centre for the Moving Image (ACMI), has an enclosed underground 'bunker' gallery built on what was originally a platform of the old Princes Bridge Station, below the northern edge of the site. Although the square has won several major architectural awards it was also dubbed the "World's Fifth Ugliest Building" by judges at *Virtual Tourist* who compared it to a bombed-out war bunker.

NOT WAVING

The iconic wave-shaped roof of Southern Cross railway station, which opened in 2006, was supposed to extend a little further north. But, in the fine tradition of major infrastructure projects not being completed exactly as intended, it does not cover the walkway between Spencer Street and the Docklands stadium. It was also cut short on the western side of the station and a flat roof built over new platforms. There were also supposed to be two office and residential blocks in the northern part of the redevelopment but, again, cost blow-outs meant they were given the chop and the site became a shopping centre instead.

LIVEABILITY

Melbourne was named the World's Most Liveable city for seven years running, from 2011 to 2018. The title was awarded by the business-oriented *The Economist* magazine's intelligence unit after surveying 173 cities around the world and measuring them in five categories: stability, healthcare, culture and environment, education, and infrastructure. After dropping to tenth, Melbourne currently ranks third in the world.

TREEMAIL

Since 2013 every tree within the City of Melbourne boundary has had its own email address. Originally intended as a way for members of the public to report a problem with an individual tree, widespread media coverage led to thousands of people from all over the world writing to the trees. The identification number and email address of each tree appears on an interactive map at http://melbourneurbanforestvisual.com.au/

LONGEST AND BUSIEST

On completion of a track extension in 2014, Melbourne tram route 75 became the longest tram line (within a single urban setting) in the world. It runs from Central Pier in the Docklands district to the eastern suburb of Vermont South and covers 22.8 kilometres. The route has gradually grown in length after starting life as a 'short-working' substitute of tram route 74. The journey today, which, coincidently, has 75 stops, takes approximately an hour and 20 minutes, sometimes longer depending on traffic conditions. The honour of being the busiest tram corridor in the world belongs to Swanston Street which has eight different tram routes (including a night service) running along it.

CASINO HEIST

Crown Casino fell victim to an elaborate 'Ocean's Eleven' style robbery in 2013 when a wealthy 'high roller' customer allegedly conspired with an employee to mark cards (thereby cheating) and somehow avoid detection by security cameras. Although the theft, believed to be in the region of $33 million, was never officially reported, Victoria Police said they were assisting the casino to recover the cash. No person has ever been arrested or charged with the robbery and casino management later said that some of the money had been returned.

LOVE UNLOCKED

In 2015, council officials removed 20,000 padlocks fixed by lovestruck couples to a pedestrian bridge over the Yarra. The worldwide craze of 'love locks' involved etching names or initials onto the locks and throwing the keys into a river. The city Lord Mayor said the extra weight had begun to affect the structure of the bridge and the wires on which they had been fixed were sagging, causing safety problems. The volume of metal keys thrown into

Love locks before they were removed.

the river was also an environmental concern. The city council asked for ideas about what to do with the locks after their removal with some eventually being used in art installations with 'love' as the subject or theme.

THUNDERSTRUCK

Melbourne is the unfortunate world capital of Thunderstorm Asthma, a medical phenomenon caused by huge amounts of pollen particles being driven by wind ahead of a heavy storm front. It is particularly severe in Victoria because particles from large areas of rye-grass crops grown in the Western and Mallee districts are sucked up as rain passes on the way to dump on Melbourne. On a single, record-breaking day in November 2016, 10 people died and 3400 were hospitalised as the result of a Thunderstorm Asthma event.

SMART PARK

Argyle Square in Carlton, became an electronic 'smart park' in 2020 when the city council began installing sensors and other hidden devices. These detect a range of activity throughout the day including how busy the park is, how many people have occupied a specific bench, the temperature in various spots, and how full the rubbish bins are. The information is published continuously on the council's *Data in the Park* webpage. Similar automated information-gathering systems have since been installed in Royal Park, and Eades Park in West Melbourne.

THE GREEK-EST

Melbourne is home to the largest community of Greek people outside Greece. According to the 2021 Australian Census, the city has more than 400,000 people of Greek descent, making it the largest Greek community after Athens and Thessaloniki and thus the third largest Greek community in the world. An official Greek 'precinct' along Lonsdale Street was designated in 1994 and the suburb of Oakleigh has been described as the "Greek-est place outside of Greece."

GRASSHOPPERING

In August 2022 researchers from the University of Melbourne released 3000 Matchstick Grasshoppers into parkland around the city in an attempt to 'renature' the environment with locally-extinct insects. The flightless grasshoppers cannot travel far — in fact they have not been able to cross the Yarra — and according to city council officials they play an important role in the natural ecosystem as a food source for other small animals

POP-UP CHURCHES

The first Anglican Prayer Book Service was held in 1835 but there were no proper church premises at the time. Baptist meetings were held in tents, Presbyterian services were held on the banks of the Yarra and then in a wooden hut, and the first Catholic mass was held in a store in Elizabeth Street. When the Scots' Church congregation split in 1884 the departing minister, Rev. Charles Strong, initially held meetings in the Temperance Hall and then the Athenaeum theatre. Even today, some Anglican congregations around central Melbourne meet in non-dedicated spaces, such as Merri Creek Anglican which meets in a school hall in Clifton Hill, and City on a Hill which holds some services in a cinema inside the Melbourne Central complex.

TUNNEL REBORN

The new pedestrian underpass between the new Metro Town Hall Station and Flinders Street Station partly uses an older, existing tunnel at Degraves Street. First opened in 1955, Campbell

Arcade was designed in an art-deco style with some small shops and included direct access to Melbourne's first department store, the Mutual Store. The store opened in 1872 but was completely rebuilt after a major fire in 1891. The underpass was prone to flooding and not well patronised. There had been an earlier plan to build a pedestrian bridge over Flinders Street to alleviate the peak period 'crush' but new traffic lights at the Swanston Street junction reduced this need. The Mutual Store closed in 1965 and was used as an adult education centre for several decades until converted into apartments.

THE MUTUAL STORE.—BEFORE THE FIRE.

The Flinders Street Mutual Store before being destroyed by fire. [*State Library of Victoria*]

Degraves Street underpass being dug, 1955. One of a number of infrastructure projects begun ahead of the 1956 Olympic Games.

W-CLASS CAFÉ

In December 2023 the William Angliss Institute in La Trobe Street installed a restored W-Class Melbourne tram as a 16-seat café and training facility for hospitality students at the college. More than 750 W-Class trams in different sub-classes were built between 1923 and 1956 with some of them still operating in 2024 as fare-free City Circle tourist trams. Many retired 'green rattlers' were given away for community use and some sold to private buyers for $1000 each on condition they were suitably re-purposed. The W-Class tram is regarded as something of a

Melbourne icon and images of it have appeared on many tourism related products and artifacts, including 'snow domes,' wall posters, and tea towels.

A classic Melbourne tram in Swanston Street, between Flinders Street and Princes Bridge in the 1930s. [*State Library of Victoria*].

FENG SHUI HEIGHTS

The tallest building in Melbourne is currently *Australia 108* in Southbank Boulevard. It has been designed to incorporate principles of Chinese Feng Shui in which there are minimal sharp angles or corners and lots of curves, and great care is taken over placement of entrances and doorways. The building makes maximum use of the number 8 which indicates good luck in Chinese culture, while the numbers 13 and 4 have been avoided because they mean bad luck in western and eastern cultures respectively.

The protruding yellow 'starburst' design, a third of the way from the top of the tower, is meant to replicate a star from the Australian national flag. The building is said to have the highest residential apartments anywhere in Australia with the largest penthouse on the 100th floor having initially sold for $25 million. Prices for the remaining 1104 apartments currently start at just under $500,000 and rise to a little over $5 million.

SHOWBAG HEAVEN

There were a record-breaking 400 'showbags' on sale at the Melbourne Royal Show in Flemington in 2023. The show, which began in 1848, is intended to "bring the country to the city" and includes displays and events featuring rural activities and livestock. The show has not run every year, having been cancelled during both World Wars when military forces requisitioned the grounds, and again in 2020-2021 due to the COVID-19 pandemic. An amusement park with a large variety of rides also operates during the show period. The showbags contain samples of products from a range of companies and the most popular ones usually contain chocolates and confectionery items.

Further reading

Annear, Robyn, *A City Lost and Found: Whelan the Wrecker's Melbourne*, Black Inc., Melbourne, 2005.

Annear, Robyn, *Adrift in Melbourne: Seven walks with Robyn Annear*, text publishing, Melbourne, 2021.

Annear, Robyn, *Corners of Melbourne*, text publishing, Melbourne, 2023.

Bate, Weston, *Essential, but Unplanned: The Story of Melbourne's Lanes*, State Library of Victoria, Melbourne, 2004.

Broome, Richard *et al*, *Remembering Melbourne, 1850–1950*, Royal Historical Society of Victoria, Melbourne, 2016.

Brown-May, Andrew & Swain, Shurlee (eds), *The Encyclopedia of Melbourne*, Cambridge University Press, Melbourne, 2005. [Also online: https://www.emelbourne.net.au/]

Cannon, Michael, *The Land Boomers*, Melbourne University Press, Melbourne, 1966.

FURTHER READING | 155

Cannon, Michael, *Old Melbourne Town Before the Gold Rush*, Loch Haven Books, Main Ridge, Victoria, 1991.

Chapman, Heather & Stillman, Judith, *Lost Melbourne*, Pavilion Books, London, 2015.

Chapman, Heather & Stillman, Judith, *Melbourne Then and Now*, Pavilion Books, London, 2016.

Davison, Graeme, *The Rise and Fall of Marvellous Melbourne*, Melbourne University Press, Melbourne, 2nd edn, 2005.

Dunston, David, *Governing the Metropolis: Politics, Technology and Social Change in a Victorian City: Melbourne 1851–1891*, Melbourne University Press, Melbourne, 1984.

Eidelson, Meyer, *Melbourne Dreaming: A Guide to Important Places of the Past and Present*, Aboriginal Studies Press, Canberra, 2014.

Fitzroy Historical Society, *Fitzroy, Melbourne's First Suburb*, Melbourne, 2014.

Haldane, Robert, *The People's Force: A History of the Victoria Police*, 3rd edn, Melbourne University Press, Melbourne, 2018. [First published 1986]

Kristin Otto, *Yarra: A diverting history of Melbourne's murky river*, text publishing, Melbourne, 2005.

Lack, John, *A History of Footscray*, Hargreen Publishing Co., Melbourne, 1991.

Macheras, Chris, *Old Vintage Melbourne,*, Scribe Publishers, Melbourne, 2021.

McCalman, Janet, *Struggletown: Portrait of an Australian Working-Class Community 1900–1965*, Melbourne University Press, Melbourne, 1984.

McCaughey, Davis, Perkins, Naomi & Trumble, Angus, *Victoria's Colonial Governors, 1839-1900*, Miegunyah Press [Melbourne University Press], Melbourne, 1993.

National Centre for Biography, Australian National University, *Australian Dictionary of Biography*, vols 1–18, Melbourne University Press, Melbourne, 1966-2012; vol 19, ANU Press, Canberra. 2021. [Also online: https://adb.anu.edu.au/]

O'Hanlon, Seamus & Luckins, Tania (eds), *Go! Melbourne in the Sixties*, Circa Books, Melbourne, 2005.

Presland, Gary, *Aboriginal Melbourne: The Lost Land of the Kulin*, Highland Press, Melbourne, 2001.

Shaw, A G L, *A History of the Port Phillip District: Victoria Before Separation*, Melbourne University Press, Melbourne, 1996.

U'Ren, Nancy & Turnbull, Noel, *A History of Port Melbourne*, Oxford University Press, Melbourne, 1983.

Wilson, Dean, *The Beat: Policing a Victorian City*, Circa Books, Melbourne, 2006.

Yule, Peter, *Carlton, A History*, Melbourne University Press, Melbourne, 2004.

Index

3DB 90, 98
aeroplane 85, 108, 69, 75, 118,
Age, The 25, 62,
Albert [ship] 18
Albert Park Lake 38
Albert, Prince 19, 38
ambulances 70, 94
American Civil War 36
Amorphophallus titanum 37
Anglican x, 12, 149
Anguilla australis 37
ANZ Bank 68, 100
Aquarium x, 118
Archer [horse] 32
Argus, The ix, 13, 32, 58, 115, 118, 119
Arnott's 24
Arthur, Governor George 4
Arthur's Seat 3
Arts Centre 40, 133
Australia 108 162-163

Australian Biscuit Company 24
Australian Rules Football 27, 43, 83, 89, 115
Australian Secret Intelligence Service 134
Bank Place 11
banks x, 66, 71, 100, 111,
Barrow, Louise 48,
Barry, Sir Redmond 22, 49
Bass Strait 2
Batman Hill 7, 9, 10
Batman, Henry 4
Batman, John xii, 4, 5, 6, 7, 10, 12
Batman, John [junior] 14
Batman, William 4
Batmania 5, 6
Battle of Trafalgar 130
Baudin, Nicholas 2
Bearbrass xi, 6
Beatles, The 124
beer 13, 66, 69, 76, 128

Bellerophon, HMS 130
Bent, Sir Thomas 82
Black War/Black Line 4
Blamey, Sir Thomas 29
Block Arcade, The 31-32
Blue Jackets 79-80
Boethius' De musica 27
Bonaparte, Emperor Napoléon 2, 130
boomerang arch 116, 117
Botanic Gardens 14, 37, 95
Bourke Street 13, 34, 37, 42, 52, 53, 54, 76, 95, 96, 104, 116, 117, 138
Bourke, Governor Sir Richard 7, 8
bread 105-106
breakfast 39, 108
Brown-Out Strangler 109
bubonic plague 58
Burke and Wills 34
cable cars, see also trams 50, 54, 55, 139
Camp Murphy 110
caravanseries x
cars 81, 94-95, 135, 137
Cavalcade of Transport 132
cemeteries 14, 42, 48, 74, 131
Cerberus, HMVS 19
Chief Commissioner 21
Chinatown 35, 78
Chloé 50-51
Church of England, *see* Anglican
churches 11, 12, 34, 82, 97, 148
cinemas 38, 41, 68, 116, 149
City Baths 31
City Hatters 83

City Loop 134-135
City Police 20, 21, 42
Clapp, Francis 54
Coat of Arms 108
Cobb & Co 54
coffee x, 39, 51, 60, 74, 117, 138
Cole's Book Arcade 98
Collins Street 8, 29, 31, 34, 42, 57, 60, 69, 77-78, 98, 100, 121, 124, 131, 140
Commonwealth Naval Forces 18
Conder, Charles 63
Confederate States Navy 36
Coode: Sir John 55; canal 58; island 58
Cooper and Bailey circus 40
Cremorne Gardens 34
Cricket: club 21, 43; ground 21, 44, 110, 122
Crown Casino 111, 145
Crystal Palace 25
Cuneiform 27
cycle paths 137
Cycloramas 61
Daily News 13
Daimaru 136
Dampier, Alfred 83
Deakin, Alfred 85
Deeming, Fredrick Bayley 84-85
Degraves Street 111
detectives 35, 84
diggers 20, 23
dim sims 112
dinner 39
Docklands 8, 55, 100, 119, 144, 145
dog parade 89

INDEX | 159

Doing the Block 31-32
Doyle, Sir Arthur Conan 89
dust storm 133
Edward, Prince of Wales 51
eels 14
Elizabeth II, Queen 25, 58, 108, 118
Elizabeth Street 10, 31, 38, 48-49, 49, 71, 77, 89, 149
Emerald Hill, *see also* South Melbourne 38
escalator 135
Eureka uprising 29, 49
Exhibition Building x, 25, 26, 28, 57, 62, 80, 116
Exposition Universalle 25
Fake Digger Weddings 22-23
Fawkner, John Pascoe xi, xii, 4, 12, 13
Federal Coffee Palace 60
Federal Parliament 26, 82
Federation Square 12, 142
Federici, Frederick 59
Feng Shui 162
Fields, W. C. 37
fire brigade 53, 83
Fisherman's/Fishermans Bend 125
FitzGerald family 40
Fitzgerald, Dr Thomas 50
Flagstaff Hill 14
Flemington Racecourse 85
Flinders Street 10, 47, 54, 74, 90, 96, 151, 158
Flinders Street Station 25, 47, 49, 50, 59, 70-71, 80, 83, 102, 111, 129, 149

flooding 21, 46, 89, 160
Footscray 112
For the Term of His Natural Life 68
Ford Motors 94
Formula One Grand Prix 38
Forum Theatre 96
gaols 10, 48, 65, 82
gas lamps 30,
General Post Office x, 89
Georges department store 140
ghosts 59
Gill, S. T. 22, 32, 81
Good Friday Appeal 90, 97
Gothic Bank 100
Government House 40, 85
Governor-General 40
GPO, *see* General Post Office
Graham, Dr Billy 122
Grand Coffee Palace *see also* Windsor Hotel 51, 60
Grand National Baby Show 62-63
grass carpet 136
grasshoppers 148
Great Exhibition 26
Great Fire of Melbourne 69
Great White Fleet 79
Greek [diaspora] 148
Guillaux, Maurice 85
Halim family 51
hats: shop 83; factory 48
Herald Sun 12, 13, 90
Herald, The 91, 118
Hertz, Carl 68
Hill of Content 13
hitching post 129
Hobson's/Hobsons Bay 3, 71
Hoddle, Robert 7, 8

Holden Motors 94-96
Hotham, Governor Charles 22
Houdini 37
hulks 28
Iberia [ship] 60
Illustrated London News ix
Imperial Hotel 26
Indented Head 4
Italians 60, 83, 105
Jack the Ripper 64-65
Johnson, President Lyndon 125
Kelly, Ellen 46
Kelly, Ned 46, 49
King Street 11, 60
King, Governor Philip Gidley 2
Kulin i, 5,
La Trobe Reading Room 25, 27
Lady Nelson, HMASV 2, 3
lagoons 14, 38
Lantern [horse] 32
Launceston 4
Lawn Tennis 43
Lennox Bridge 19
life expectancy 64
lifts, hydraulic 38
Lindrum family 74, 75
List, Norman Alfred 95
Little Audrey 127
Little Bourke Street 35, 62, 78, 121
Little Collins Street 10, 62, 83, 148
liveability 144
Lloyd, Marie 37
Loch, Sir Henry x
Lonsdale Street 62, 99
love locks 148

Luna Park 84
Lyceum Club 100
MacArthur, General Douglas 29
magicians 68, 83, 138
Maribyrnong River 55, 112, 113
markets 12, 42, 43, 96, 112
Marvellous Melbourne ix, xii, 54
Mather, Emily 84
McCafé 138
Meals on Wheels 116
Melba, Nellie 57
Melbourne Advertiser 12, 13
Melbourne Central Station, *see also* Museum Station 134
Melbourne City Council 31, 42, 108, 129, 139, 147-148, 149
Melbourne Cricket Ground 21, 44, 110, 122
Melbourne Cup 32-33, 52
Melbourne Opera House, see also Tivoli Theatre 37, 68, 83, 86
Melbourne Public Library, see also State Library of Victoria 22, 27, 48
Melways 126
Menzies Hotel x, 29, 68
Mercury statue 69
Metro rail 148
Miegunyah Press 118
Mirka's 117, 121
Mitchell, David 57
Mitre Tavern 11
Mods 124
Moonee Valley racecourse 115
morgues 32, 111
motion pictures 37, 68
munitions factories 112-113

INDEX | 161

Munro, James 51
Murdoch, Rev. Patrick 82
Murray, Acting-Lieutenant John 2, 3
Museum Station, see also Melbourne Central Station 134
museums 49, 67, 69, 116, 125, 137
Mutual Store 150
Myer 99, 104, 120, 136
National Gallery of Victoria 50, 63, 128
Native Police 21
Nauru 131
Nelson HMVS 18
New South Wales 4, 113
newspapers, see *The Argus, The Age, Daily News, Daily Telegraph* [London], *The Herald, Melbourne Advertiser, Port Phillip Gazette, Port Phillip Patriot, Punch, Sun News-Pictorial*
Nine-by-Five Exhibition 63
No. 2 Goods Shed 8
nursery 102-103
Old Mint 21
Olympia 40-41,
Olympic Games 118, 120, 151
Ormond, Francis 58
Paris End, The 121, 140
Parliament House x, 26-27, 44, 72, 97, 116
Parwill, *see* Vegemite
Péron, François 2
Persian Rug of Light 128
Peters Ice Cream 24
Pflanz, SS 86

Pleasant Hill 7
Point Gellibrand 14
police 20, 21, 41-42, 52, 61, 62, 63, 78, 81, 88, 91, 92, 95, 105, 113, 123, 131, 134, 146
Police Paddock, *see also* Melbourne Cricket Ground 121
Port Jackson 2
Port Melbourne, *see also* Sandridge 23, 24, 80, 86, 137
Port Phillip Bay 2, 3, 4, 38
Port Phillip Gazette 13
Port Phillip Patriot 13
Presbyterian 11, 76, 82, 149
Presley, Elvis 131
Price, Inspector-General John 29-30
Prince's Bridge Hotel *see also* Young and Jackson's 10, 69
Prince's Bridge Station 48, 143, 156
Prince's/Princes Bridge 19, 109, 126
Princes Court 40
Princess/Princess's Theatre 59
Punch 51
punt [water] 19, 27-28, 137
Punt Road 27
Puppy Dog Corner 98
Queen's/Queens Bridge 5, 14, 84, 126
Queenie [elephant] 79
radio masts 90
Railway Pier, *see also* Station Pier 24-25
Railway Viewing Platform 138
Rebecca 4

Red Cross
Ress, Leon 121
Rickards, Harry 68
RMIT University 58
Roberts, Tom 63
Roman Catholic x, 148
Roosevelt, President Theodore 80
Royal Australian Navy 18
Royal Children's Hospital 90, 97
Royal Mail Hotel 52-53
Royal Park 34, 111, 148
Royal Show 164
Rubinstein, Helena 77-78
Russell Street 10, 34, 76, 77, 78, 88
Russell, Robert 8
Sala, George Augustus ix-xii
Salisbury Cathedral 12
Salvation Army 47
Sandridge, *see also* Port Melbourne 23, 24, 38
Scienceworks 48, 67, 137
Scots' Church 11, 34, 57, 149
Scottish [diaspora] 71-72
Seaworks Maritime Precinct 32
sewer 67
Sharpies 124
Shell House 138
Shenandoah, CSS 36
Shepherd, William 47
Sheraton Hotel 134
Shing, Fook 35
Showbags 163
Shrimpton, Jean 123
Shrine of Remembrance 101-102
six o'clock swill 128

Skeleton Army 47
Smart Park 147-148
Smileaway Club 90
South Melbourne, *see also* Emerald Hill 38
Southern Cross Station, see also Spencer Street Station 7, 48, 119, 132, 139, 143
Spencer Street 8, 54, 69, 89, 144
Spencer Street Station, *see also* Southern Cross Station 49, 122, 132
SPHAIRISTIKE 43
Spotswood 49, 67, 137
Spring Street 28, 34, 44, 51, 62, 70, 129, 134, 136
St James Old Cathedral 11
St Kilda Road 29, 40, 41, 101, 128, 133, 137
St Paul's Cathedral 12, 143
State Library of Victoria, *see also* Melbourne Public Library 22, 25, 27, 138
Station Pier, *see also* Railway Pier 24
Stonnington 40
Streeton, Arthur 63
Sun News-Pictorial 123
Swallow & Ariell Steam Biscuit Company 23-24
Swallow, Thomas 23
swing basin 84, 100
Tango [dance] 86
Tasmania *see also* Van Dieman's Land 4, 13, 75, 89
Taylor, Squizzy 88
Telegraph, Daily [London] ix

television 118, 123, 125, 126
Terre Napoléon 2
The Land of the Golden Fleece ix
theatres 34, 37, 59, 63, 68, 86, 89, 96, 149
Thompson, Eliza 4, 10
Thunderstorm Asthma 147
tigers 128
Tilly Aston 140
Tirtschke, Alma 91
titan arum 37
Tivoli Theatre, *see also* Melbourne Opera House 37-38
toilets 76-77
Trades Hall 88
trams, *see also* cable cars 55, 139, 151-152
Treasury Gardens 129
Treemail 144
tunnels 26, 67, 111, 149-150
Twain, Mark 68
University High School 59
University of Melbourne x, 22-23, 59, 100, 101, 103-104, 118, 148
Van Dieman's Land 4
Vegemite 93-94
Victoria [ship] 18
Victoria amazonia 37
Victoria Barracks 29
Victoria Club 130
Victoria, Queen 18, 38, 40

von Mueller, Ferdinand 37
waggonettes x
Wallace [lion] 83-84
water lily 37
Water Tower Clock 49-50
West Melbourne Swamp 55-56
Westgate 67, 137
William Street xi, 21, 42, 136
William's Creek 48
Williamstown 14, 18, 21, 32, 60, 80, 130
Wilson's Promontory 2
Windsor Hotel, *see also* The Grand Coffee Palace 51, 70
Wingfield, Wallace 43
Wirth family 40-41
Women's Hospital 100
Woniora SS 87
World War I 86, 88, 95, 102, 113, 128
World War II 25, 29, 87, 103, 108, 109, 111, 112
Wurundjeri i, 7
Wurundjeri Woi-wurrung i
Yarra Falls 14, 15
Yarra River xi, xii, 5, 7, 11, 14, 15, 28, 38, 46, 47, 55, 56, 67, 84, 111, 137, 146, 149
Yarro-yarro 7
Young and Jackson's 10, 50, 69
zoo 52, 79, 84, 99